Did Y

KING

A M

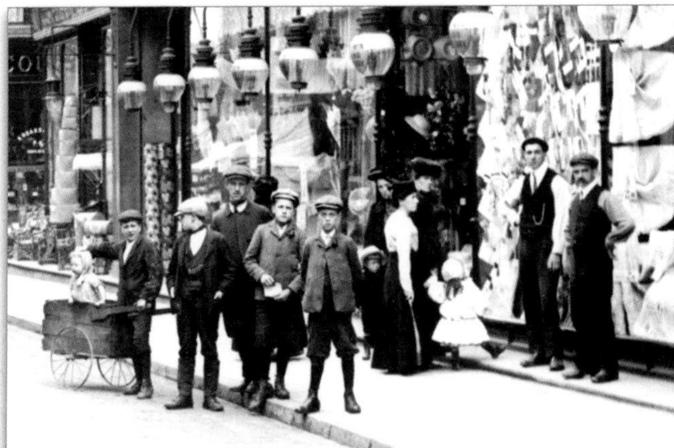

Compiled by Julia Skinner

With particular reference to the work of Adrian G Parker and Bryan Howling

THE FRANCIS FRITH COLLECTION

www.francisfrith.com

Based on a book first published in the United Kingdom in 2004 by The Francis Frith Collection®

Hardback edition published exclusively for Identity Books in 2009 ISBN 978-1-84589-400-9

British Library Cataloguing in Publication Data

Did You Know? King's Lynn - A Miscellany
Compiled by Julia Skinner
With particular reference to the work of Adrian G Parker and Bryan Howling

The Francis Frith Collection
Frith's Barn, Teffont,
Salisbury, Wiltshire SP3 5QP
Tel: +44 (0) 1722 716 376
Email: info@francisfrith.co.uk
www.francisfrith.com

Printed and bound in Singapore

Front Cover: **KING'S LYNN, HIGH STREET 1908** 60023p

The colour-tinting is for illustrative purposes only, and is not intended to be historically accurate

AS WITH ANY HISTORICAL DATABASE, THE FRANCIS FRITH ARCHIVE IS CONSTANTLY BEING CORRECTED AND IMPROVED, AND THE PUBLISHERS WOULD WELCOME INFORMATION ON OMISSIONS OR INACCURACIES

CONTENTS

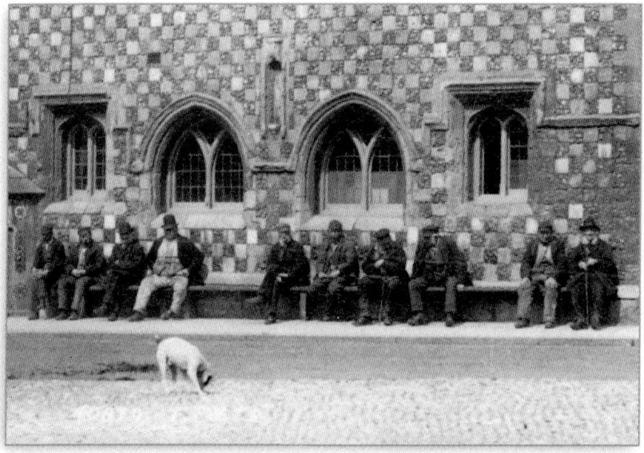

INTRODUCTION

Centuries ago the Wash was much larger than it is today. Situated on its south-east corner, King's Lynn, known to its inhabitants as Lynn, was built on the edge of the sea, probably with help from the Romans, and later from the Dutch, who were expert in cutting dykes. From ancient times it was always a populous and flourishing seaport, borough and market town.

All the navigable rivers in the area met at Lynn's harbour. One of the early industries of the area was salt production, and during the Anglo-Saxon era there were fifty salt pans operating. Trade in other commodities developed during the Middle Ages, including furs, cloth, farm produce, fish, wine and wood, bringing in merchants and buyers from home and abroad. From the 16th century more merchants and traders came into Lynn, and a huge manufacturing industry developed, including textiles, weaving, tanning, shoemaking, baking, milling, shipbuilding, ropemaking and goldsmithing.

During the Civil War the leading lights of Lynn supported the Royalist cause and seized control of the town to hold it for the king. The town's defences were put to the test against 17,000 Parliamentarian soldiers of the Eastern Association, and it was put under siege for almost three weeks; when the town surrendered, a fine of £3,200 was levied to alleviate the suffering of the townsfolk. It is not certain whether it was a Dutch ship lying in the harbour of the army in West Lynn who took pot shots at St Margaret's Church during the siege, but whoever the culprits were, they damaged the spire and shot off various crosses, and a16lb cannonball went through a west window and damaged a pillar. The cannonball can now be seen suspended from the roof at the entrance to Hampton Court in Nelson Street.

In the 19th century the ideal trading conditions experienced by the merchants of Lynn started to come adrift with the development of the railway system. The merchants' natural reliance on trade by sea, which had lasted over hundreds of years, was virtually wiped out by the railway. Ships and boats were spending more time in port than at sea because their precious cargoes were now on railway trucks, being sent more quickly (and arriving fresher) to every quarter of the country. Another factor was the annual port dues, which exceeded all others apart from London, Bristol, Liverpool and Hull. However, the situation was alleviated somewhat when steam ships took over from the slower sailing boats. Two new docks were built to capture the trade, and huge sheds, warehouses and grain stores were erected, and railway lines were laid right up to the quayside.

The town has grown and changed over the years, but it still has two medieval churches and the two market places, as well as two guildhalls and a fortified gate. The delightful Custom House, now an emblem for the town, was built in Charles II's reign, and many fine buildings have been constructed in the 300 years since then. Major changes took place in the 19th century, and even more in the 20th. Now King's Lynn can proudly look back on over 800 years of life and growth since it was given its first charter by King John in 1204.

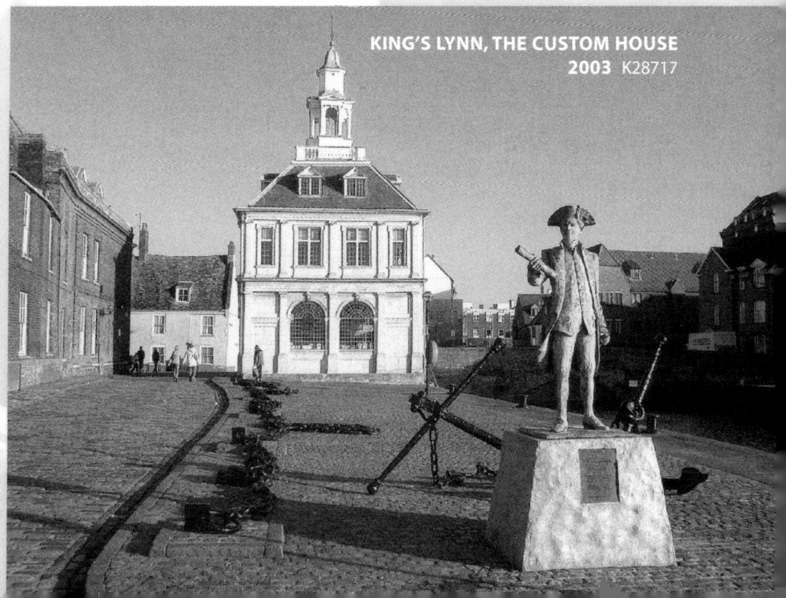

KING'S LYNN, THE CUSTOM HOUSE
2003 K28717

NORFOLK WORDS AND PHRASES

'Afront' - in front.

'Ahind' - behind.

'Atwin' - between.

'Bishy barney bee' - a ladybird.

'Dew you keep a troshin!' - carry on with the threshing (or harvesting), often used as a way of saying 'Goodbye', or 'Look after yourself'.

'Dodman' - a snail.

'Dudder' - to shiver.

'Dwile' - a floor cloth.

'Harnser' - a heron.

'I'll get wrong!' - I'll get told off!

'Lollop' - to move along slowly.

'Luggy' - deaf.

'Lummox' - a clumsy or awkward person.

'Mardle' - to gossip or chat.

'Mavish' - a thrush.

'Mawkin' - a scarecrow.

'Mawther' - a young woman.

'On the huh' - slanted, not level or straight.

'Squit' - talking nonsense.

'Titty-totty' - very small.

'Uhmtie-tump' - a mole hill.

'Warmint' - vermin, or a varmint, a troublesome person.

HAUNTED KING'S LYNN

The basement of the public library is said to be haunted, and many staff have felt very uneasy when working there.

It is said that the mark of the Devil's hoofprint can be seen in Devil's Alley. According to an old folk tale, the Devil arrived in Lynn by ship and went ashore to gather some souls. A local priest followed him to this alley, and used prayers and holy water to drive the Devil away. The Devil was so annoyed at being foiled in his plan that he stamped his foot hard on the ground before going back to his ship, and the imprint can still be seen.

For many years Queen Isabella, mother of Edward III, was kept prisoner at Castle Rising near Lynn, for conspiring with her lover to murder her husband, Edward II. When her son became king, he had his mother imprisoned in the castle for the rest of her life, and her lover was killed. Isabella is believed to have gone mad there, and it is said that her ghostly shrieks can still be heard ringing around the castle walls at night.

A haunted secret tunnel is said to link Castle Rising with Red Mount Chapel at St James Park in Lynn (see photograph K28004 on page 51). The story goes that one day a drunken fiddler rashly decided to explore the tunnel, taking his dog with him. He was never seen again, but the sound of ghostly fiddle music can be heard in the area, as well as the whimpering of his dog, desperate to get out of the tunnel.

The Duke's Head in Tuesday Market Place has several ghost stories associated with it. One says that Room 18 was for some time haunted by the ghostly moaning of a man who died there after a suicide attempt. Another concerns the ghost of a mysterious woman dressed in red, and yet another is a report of a female ghost which may be that of a maid who poisoned her mistress and was executed for her crime.

KING'S LYNN MISCELLANY

Frederick Savage (1828–97) is commemorated by a statue in Guanock Terrace, just inside the South Gates, erected in 1892. He was a Norfolk 'machine maker' who became a mechanical engineer. He started in Lynn in 1850 making agricultural implements, and finally expanded into a new works on Estuary Road in 1873. His steam-powered machinery included fairground rides and he held the patent for 'gallopers'.

The new public library was built in 1904–05, having attracted a large donation from Andrew Carnegie, a Scottish-American steel magnate who was concerned to provide better libraries. He was invited to the opening in 1905, and is thought to have assumed that King Edward VII would also appear since he had also given a (modest) sum, but this did not happen.

The River Great Ouse runs from the town to the sea in a man-made channel. The Marsh Cut, excavated in 1850–52, is 162 metres wide and two miles long. Beyond that a training wall takes the Lynn Channel through Vinegar Middle and Bull Dog Sands into the Wash.

The river upstream also flows in a man-made channel, cutting off the Saddlebow loop out to Eau Brink and Pullover, at Islington Hall. Completed in 1821, the River Cut increased the velocity of the river and thus its ability to carry silt away through the port, reducing the pumping levels from inland drainage districts.

The estuary can still be traced by the Old Eastern and Western seabanks, which are now public paths from Loke and Crossbank Roads. Old North Lynn used to be on the west bank. The docks were built in the former estuary – Alexandra Dock in 1869 and Bentinck Dock in 1883. The Pink House, on Estuary Road, has a coronet and letter P on the front (the Duke of Portland held a share in the reclamation project).

KING'S LYNN, THE QUAY 1898 40893

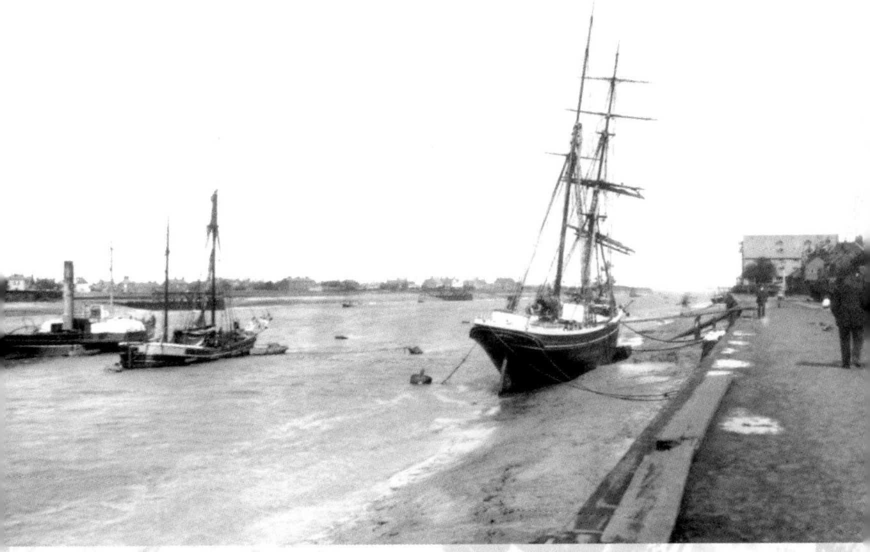

St Margaret's Church has two clocks – the bigger one, on the bell tower, tells the time; the smaller one in the southwest tower was originally a moon dial made in 1681 by Thomas Tue, who is commemorated at 51 High Street. It is now an electric clock that marks 'Lynn high tide'.

King's Lynn is one of only four towns in the country to have four maces. This ceremonial staff is descended from a medieval weapon (a spiked club) and was a symbol of the defence given to civic leaders when performing their public duties. It had become a ceremonial item by the time corporations were created, in the Tudor period. The four maces at Lynn are in silver-gilt, and were made in 1711 by a London goldsmith, Benjamin Pyne.

Bridges are relatively recent structures in Lynn. There have been four – a wooden bridge from 1821 to 1873, an iron bridge from 1873 to 1925 (kept in place for driving animals across until 1942), a concrete bowstring bridge from 1925 to 1969, and the present road bridge, opened in 1970. In addition, the southern bypass bridge was built shortly after this, close to the position of the former railway bridge.

The names of the Saxon hundreds (ancient division of a county) were Freebridge Lynn, to the east of the river, and Marshland Lynn, to the west. The bridge was at Wiggenhall St Germans, where the river narrowed. These administrative names survived until 1974, as local government names for the rural districts of Marshland and Freebridge.

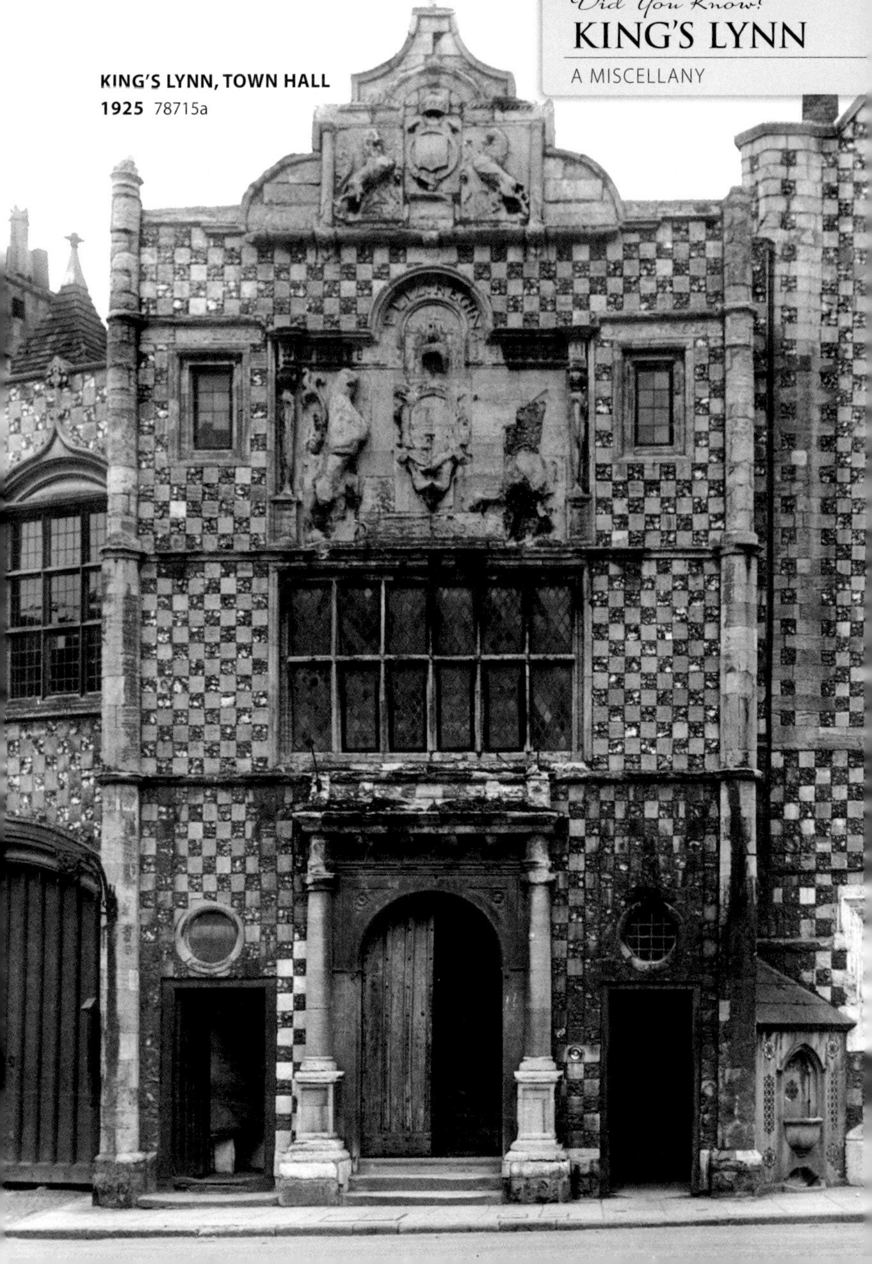

KING'S LYNN, TOWN HALL
1925 78715a

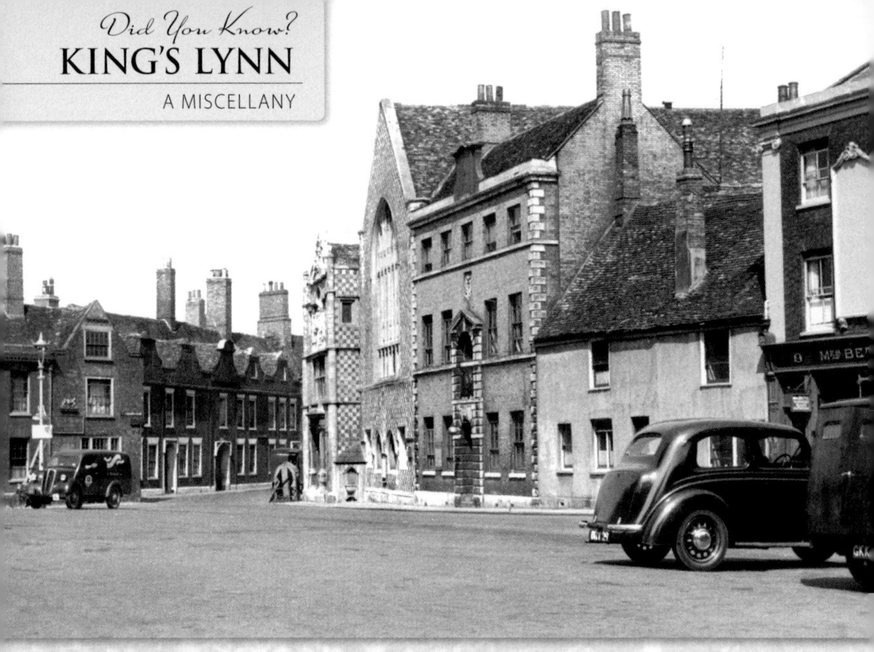

KING'S LYNN, SATURDAY MARKET PLACE AND GUILDHALL c1955 K28025

The Hanseatic League was an alliance of German towns who, from c1230, combined to obtain preferential trading rights and to protect each other's goods and shipping. The leading towns were Lubeck, Hamburg and Bremen, together with Rostock, Stettin, Danzig and other communities from the Baltic to Flanders and Bergen. They obtained rights to trade in Lynn in 1271, but had to do so through locally-based merchants.

The Hanseatic Steelyard at Lynn is the only surviving building of its kind in England, at St Margaret's House and the Registry Office off South Quay. It was given to the German cities in 1475, as part of the terms of the Peace of Utrecht (1474). Although there were Hanseatic traders in many ports, identified as Kontor, there were only ever four permanent bases owned by the Hanse. The Lynn base had closed by the 1590s, but was sold only in 1751.

KING'S LYNN, NELSON STREET 1908 60025

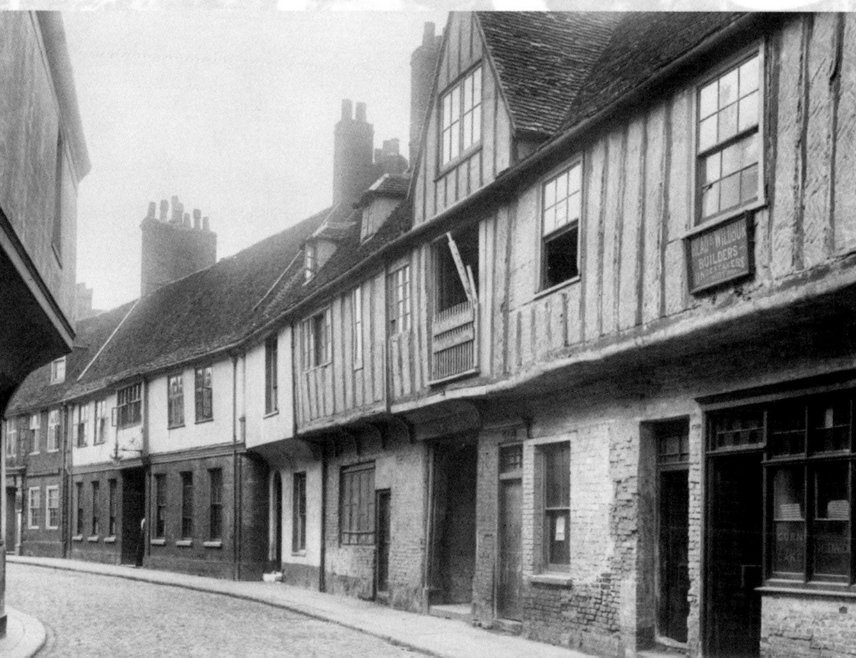

The name of Vancouver is best known as the major city on Canada's Pacific coast, but there is another Vancouver in the nearby US state of Washington, close to Portland, Oregon. The origin of the name is Captain George Vancouver RN (of Lynn), who undertook surveying voyages of the Pacific northwest coast. He was sent by the Admiralty to prepare navigation charts, from the Columbia river to Alaska, mainly in 1793–95. A statue was erected in his hometown in 2000, beside the Custom House where his father was Deputy Collector.

The town Charters include details of the grants of rights to hold fairs and markets. The Saturday and Tuesday markets remain a part of the town scene, but there is now only one fair, the Mart, beginning on St Valentine's Day each year. By the mid 19th century the trading purpose of the fair had largely disappeared and been replaced by entertainment. The Mart, now opened by the Mayor on 14 February every year and lasting for 14 days, marks the start of the season for the Showmen's Guild in England.

Whale fishing from Lynn started after the passing of the Greenland Whale Fishery Act in 1771, which encouraged investment. By 1784 there were five ships based in the town, making the annual four-month voyage, and the trade continued on into the 1820s. Whale oil was used in vast quantities for domestic lighting, in preference to candles, before town gas existed. Reminders of the industry live on in the 'Greenland Fishery' inn (a house in Bridge Street) and part of the Nar river bank known as Blubberhouse Creek.

On King's Staithe Square stands the first purpose-built banking house, of 1789. This was built for Birkbeck, Gurney and Cresswell's Bank – well-known local families – and eventually became part of Barclay's Bank. Another similar banking hall can be seen on the North Brink at Wisbech. Other banks had existed since the early 18th century, based with the leading merchants.

KING'S LYNN, HIGH STREET c1955 K28035

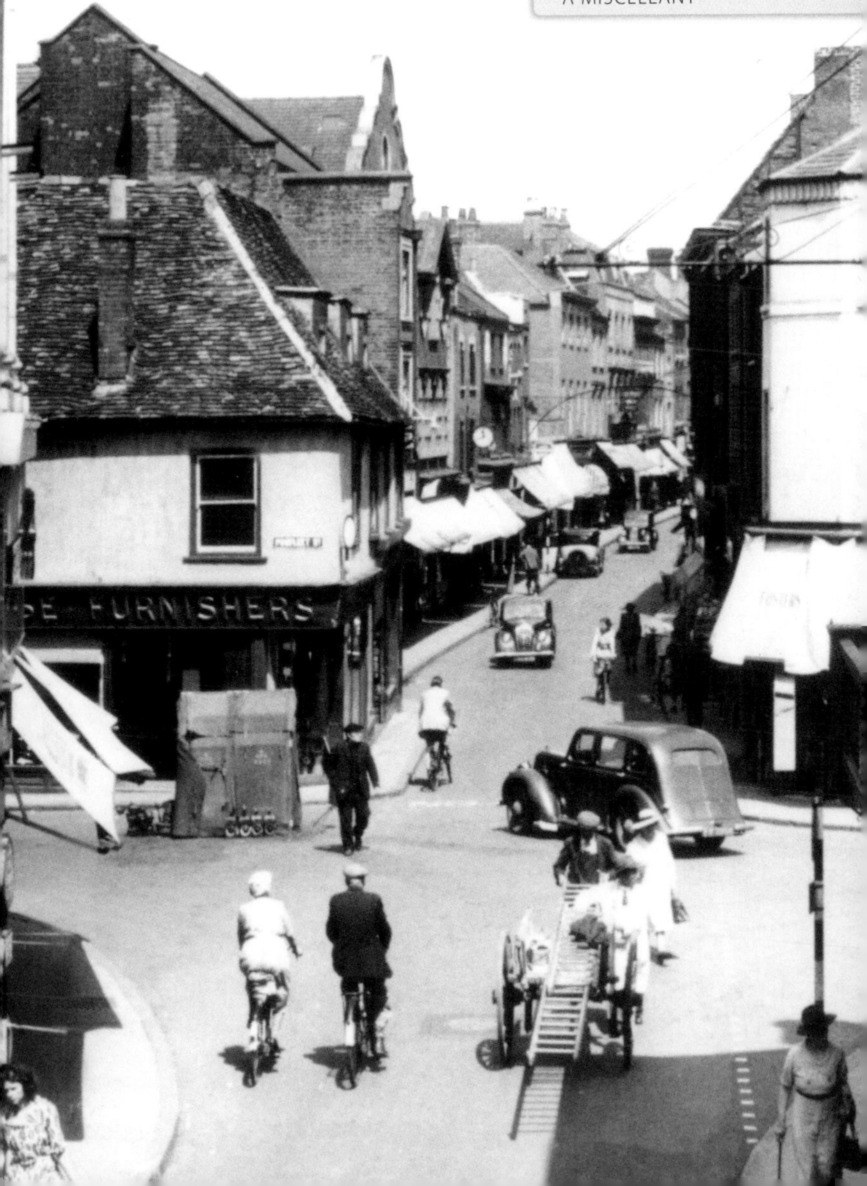

KING'S LYNN, HIGH STREET 1908 60024

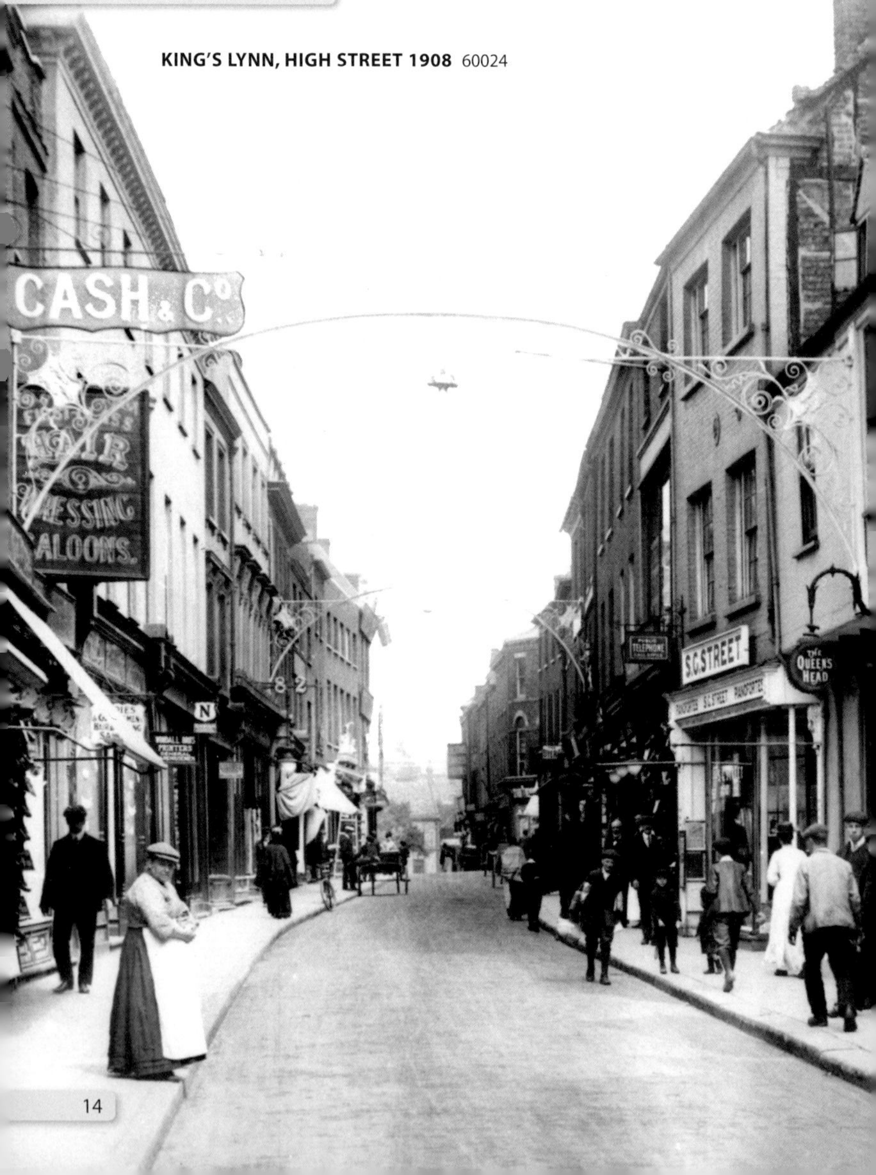

Punishments (including hangings) were carried out at both Market Places, although some executions took place at South Gates. Petty criminals of all sorts were locked into the pillories and stocks in the market places, where they were exposed to public abuse and humiliation. Two particularly ghastly executions occurred in 1531 and 1730. In the first, a maidservant, convicted of murdering her mistress, was repeatedly lowered into boiling water until she died. In the second, the wrongdoer was burned at the stake. Just as gruesome was the hanging of two children for theft in 1708 – which appalled local opinion.

King John lost his 'treasure' – his jewellery and household goods – 'in the Wash' on 12 October 1216. His convoy of baggage carts was using the short cut to Lincolnshire from Lynn, across the river mouths and along the banks of the reclaimed silt lands. This was a regular road for those travelling with local guides who knew the firmest ground. The tide closed over King John's treasure somewhere between Walpole Cross Keys and Long Sutton.

Gaywood is much older than Lynn, having been an important Saxon manor, which happened to be owned by a bishop in 1066. In front of the Hall there was a giant oak tree that was one of the meeting places for the 'Thing' – the assembly of Saxon freemen from the hundred of Freebridge Lynn. The bishop's house was within a double moat, and was fortified by Bishop Despencer in 1388.

A 'palace' of the Bishop of Norwich remained at Gaywood until 1536, when Henry VIII enforced an exchange of lands. The later owners lived elsewhere and by the 1690s the house was in ruins, but a farmhouse was built about 1693 for the Thoresby family. In 1783 Philip Case built a new farmhouse, and in 1849 that house was demolished and the present Hall built for the Bagge family.

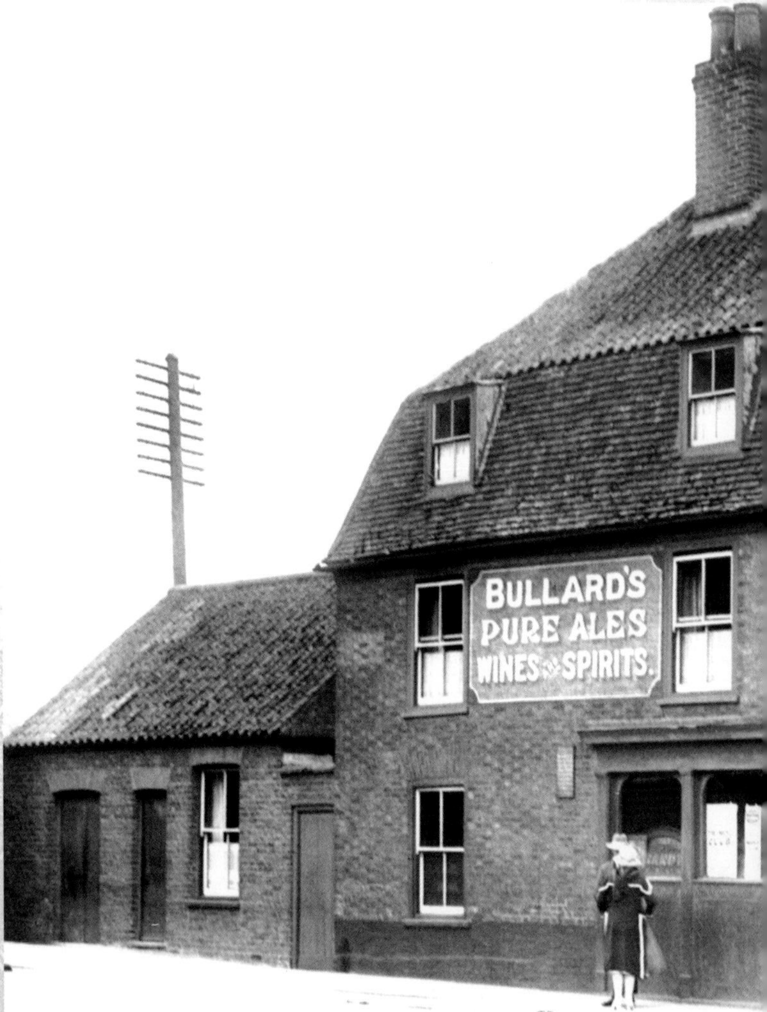
BULLARD'S
PURE ALES
WINES SPIRITS.

KING'S LYNN, THE HONEST LAWYER INN 1925 78717

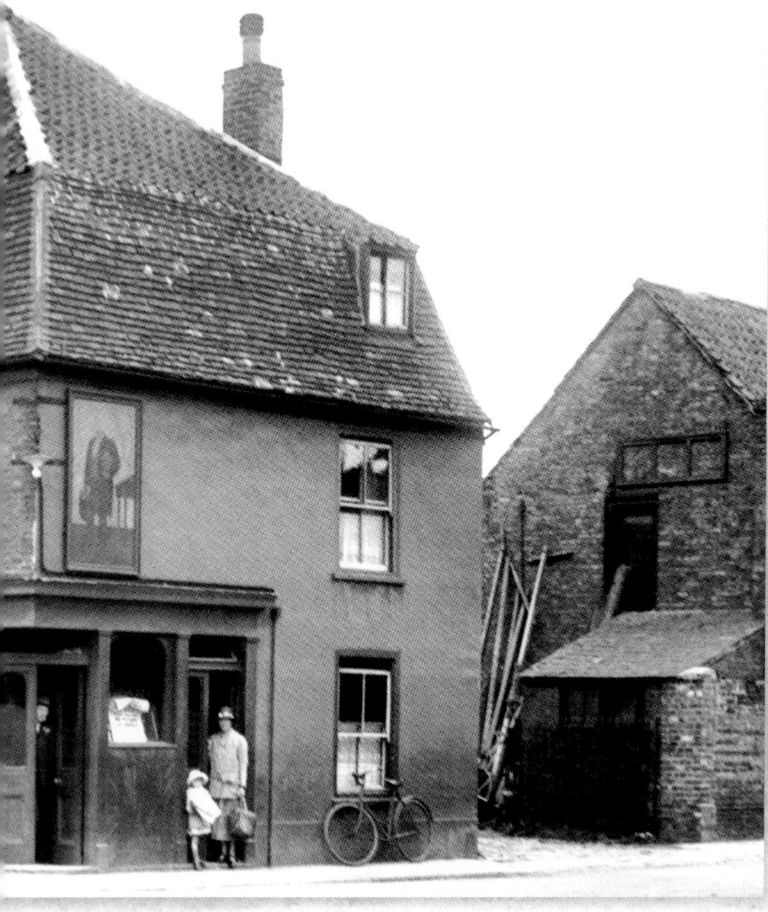

KING'S LYNN, TUESDAY MARKET PLACE 1898 40886

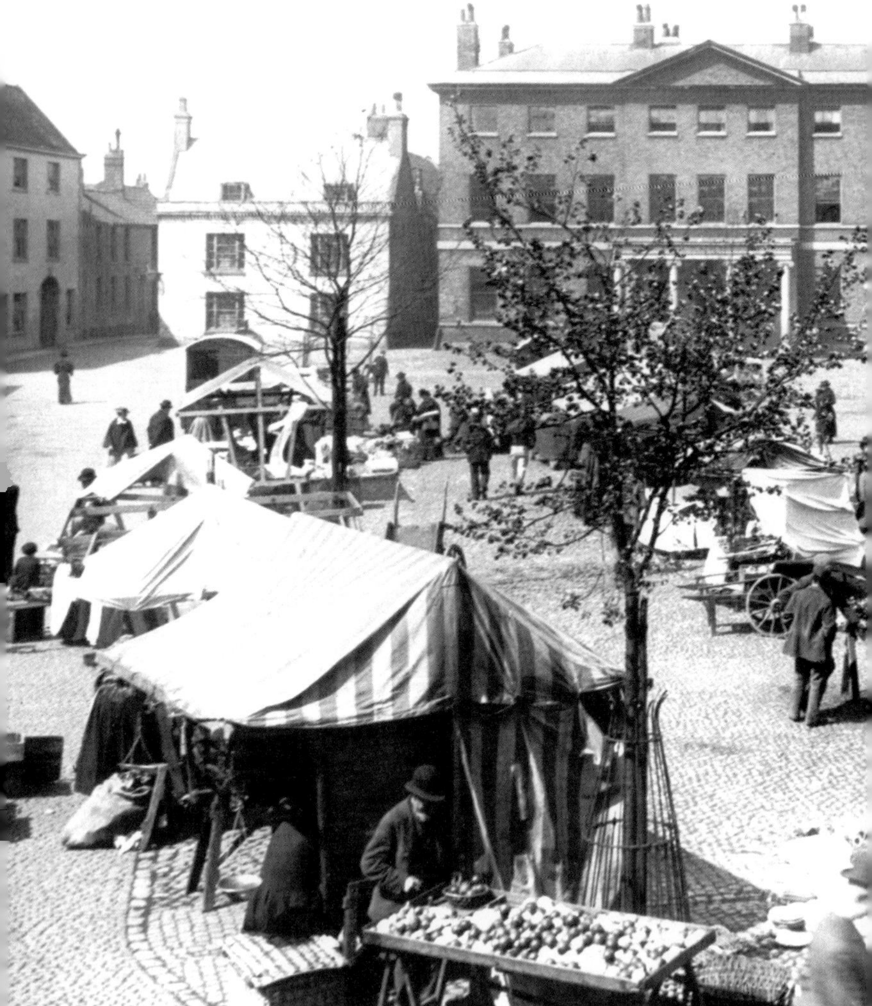

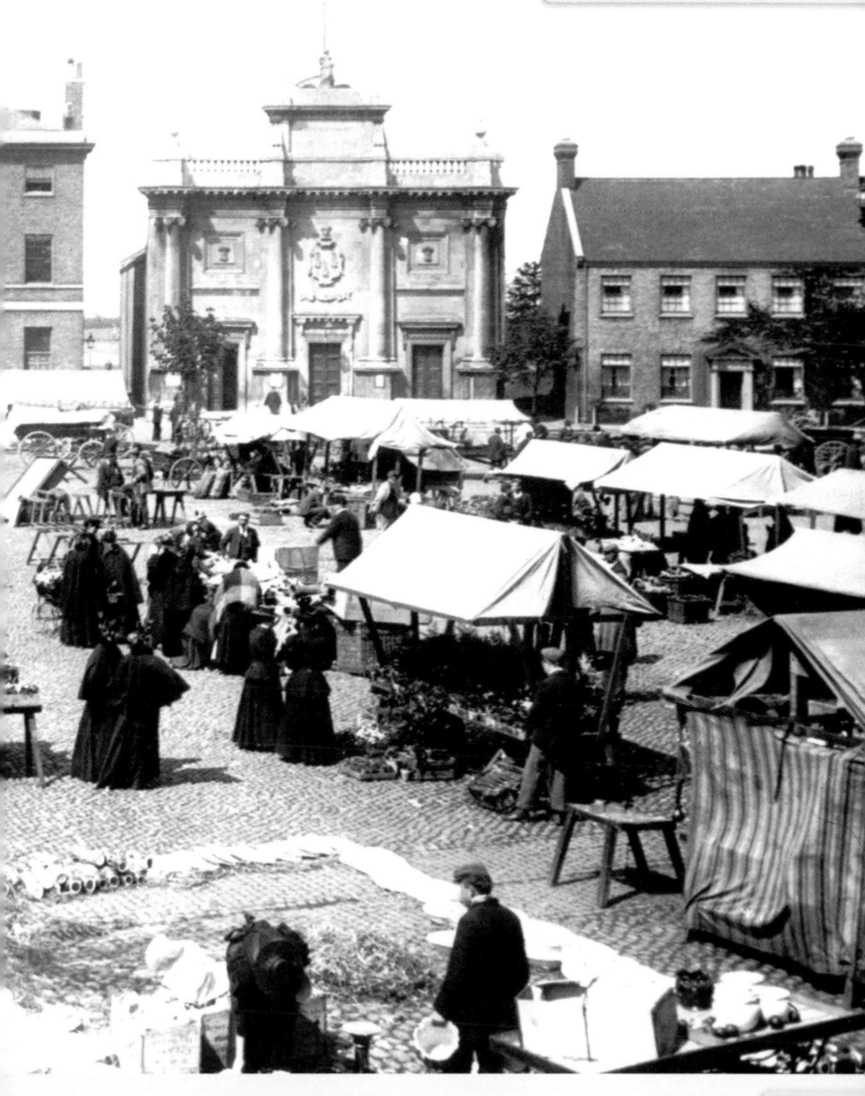

Part of the Gaywood Hall estate can still be seen at the 'Wildfowler' pub, opened in 1975, and before then at Fairstead Farmhouse, built in 1828. The nearest houses, in Regent's Park, are on the site of the estate sawmills and workshops. Just to the west is Cottage Row, originally ten cottages built c1780. Hall Lodge was built by the last Bagge to live at the Hall, in 1920. The Old Rectory, associated with the Hall for generations, appears to be mainly 1760–1806, but includes traces from before 1670.

In Gaywood there is a significant brick building, called Bishop's Terrace. This is completely misnamed, however, and was nothing to do with bishops, having been built before 1486 by John Deane, a merchant seeking a suburban house away from Lynn. The building still has Renaissance details from the 17th century, having been damaged and repaired after the Civil War siege of 1643.

Highgate is now a small housing street near the 'Hob in the Well' public house. It was the first suburban housing area outside the walls, which is what 'suburban' means. Built in the 1820s and 1830s, it was in the parish of Gaywood and was incorporated within the town only in 1835. The streets were called Front Row, Double Row, Garden Row, Stag Place and Exhibition Terrace, and the area was cleared for redevelopment in 1955.

St James's chapel in Lynn was a 'daughter' church of St Margaret's. Although it is only 400 metres away, St James' probably served a farming community within the sea banks, rather than the townspeople nearer the river. The chapel was despoiled very soon after the Reformation in 1538, and treated as part of the confiscated property rather than a church in which parishioners had any rights. Cartloads of tiles and bricks were sold, before the ruins were fitted out as a Poor Law factory, and after 1681 as the Workhouse.

KING'S LYNN, ST MARGARET'S CHURCH c1900 28763

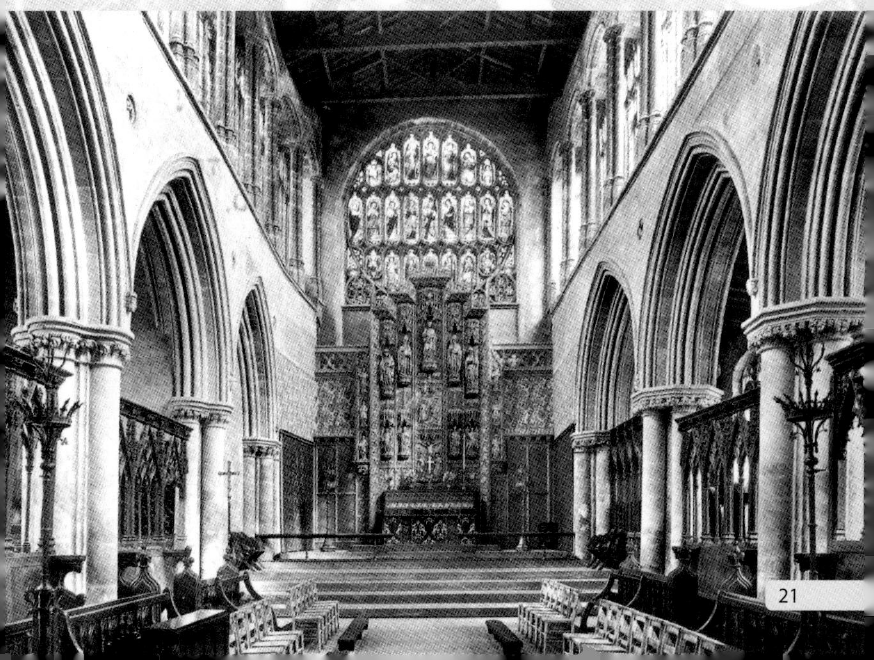

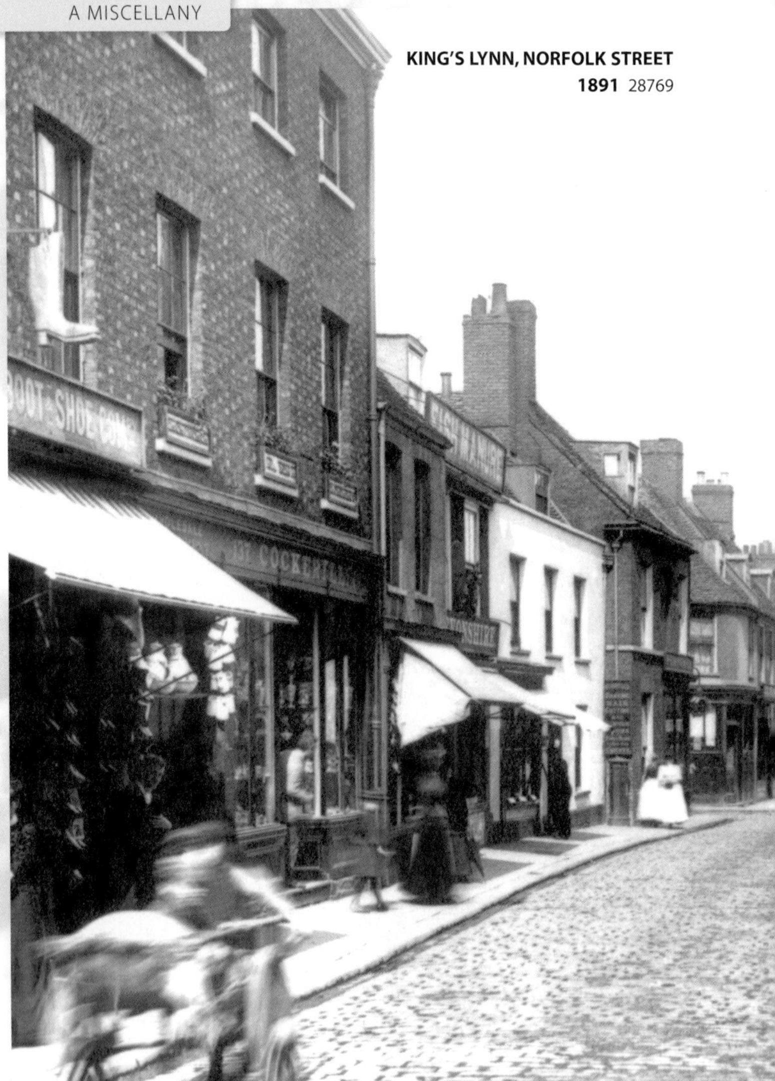

KING'S LYNN, NORFOLK STREET
1891 28769

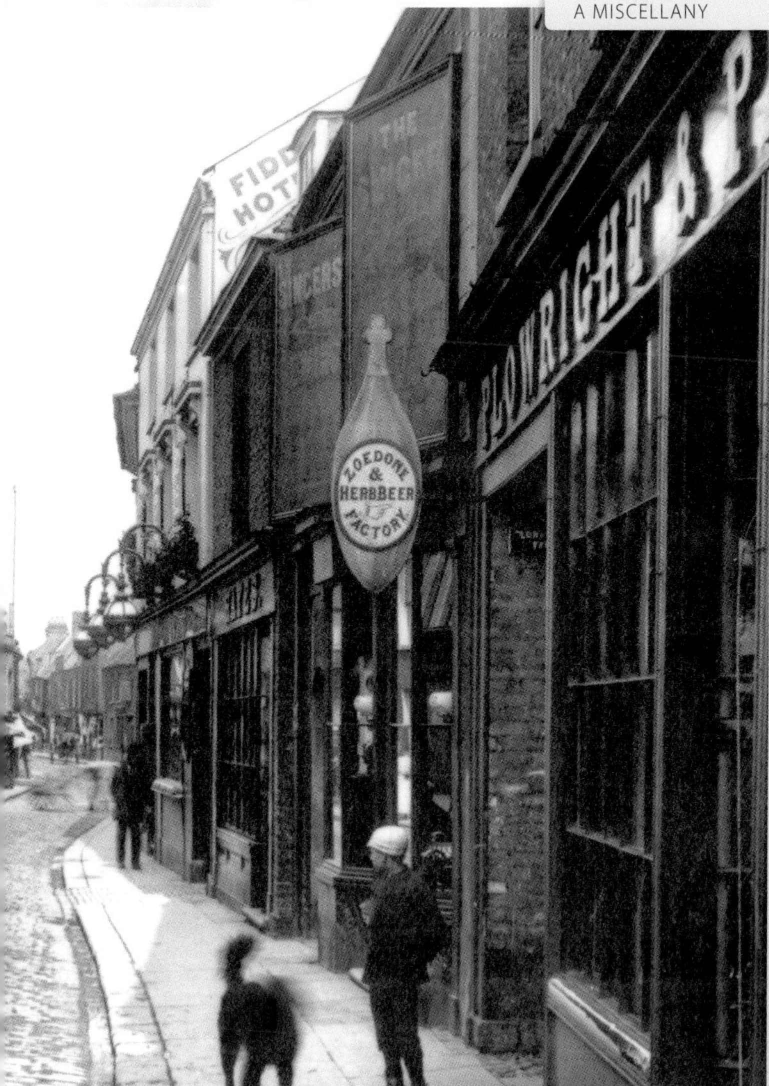
ZOEDONE
&
HERB BEER
FACTORY
PLOWRIGHT & P

The South Gates at Lynn are always known locally in the plural, no doubt a reference to the gates themselves, rather than the gatehouse. The gatekeeper was a civic officer in medieval times, and he needed to be capable of writing and keeping accounts of the tolls collected. Later the job must have become more like that of a council superintendent, for included in its title was 'Keeper of the Muckhills' – the organiser of waste cleansing.

The South Gates has a misleading plaque (built into it in the early 1900s) with the date 1520 on it. This relates only to the refacing of the building in secondhand stone, and work done to the interior arches. Most of the gatehouse was built of brick in 1437–40, on the site of at least one earlier building. There has been a gatehouse here since before 1300.

The East Gates were at Littleport bridge – still visible under the modern bridge from the park in Kettlewell Lane. A gate must have been amongst the earliest defences in 1267, but the gate illustrated in 1741 had been built in about 1440. It was in a different style from the South Gates and had a lower arch; it was demolished in 1800. The beer house in the side of the gate was rebuilt as the 'Hob in the Well'. It is a myth that the gate was demolished in order to move big pictures from Houghton Hall to Russia in 1779!

KING'S LYNN, SOUTH GATES 1891 28760

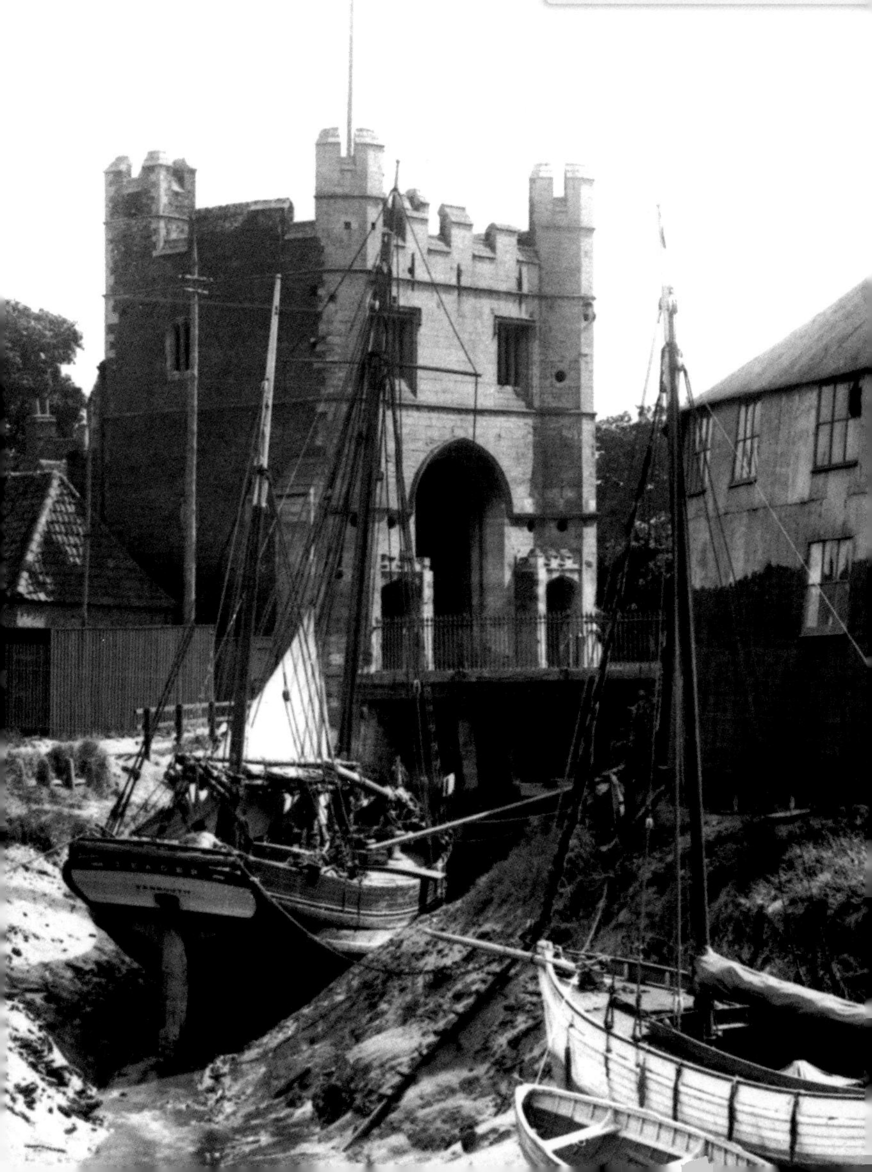

The porch to the Town Hall has become known as the 'Elizabethan Porch', because the central royal arms are those of Elizabeth I. However, this plaque was taken from the 'house of industry' in St James' chapel, and the whole of the porch was new in 1624, in the reign of James I. To add to the confusion, the upper tablet depicts the royal arms of Charles I (reigned 1625–49), but was altered by Mayor Wharton in 1664.

KING'S LYNN, THE TOWN HALL 1898 40879

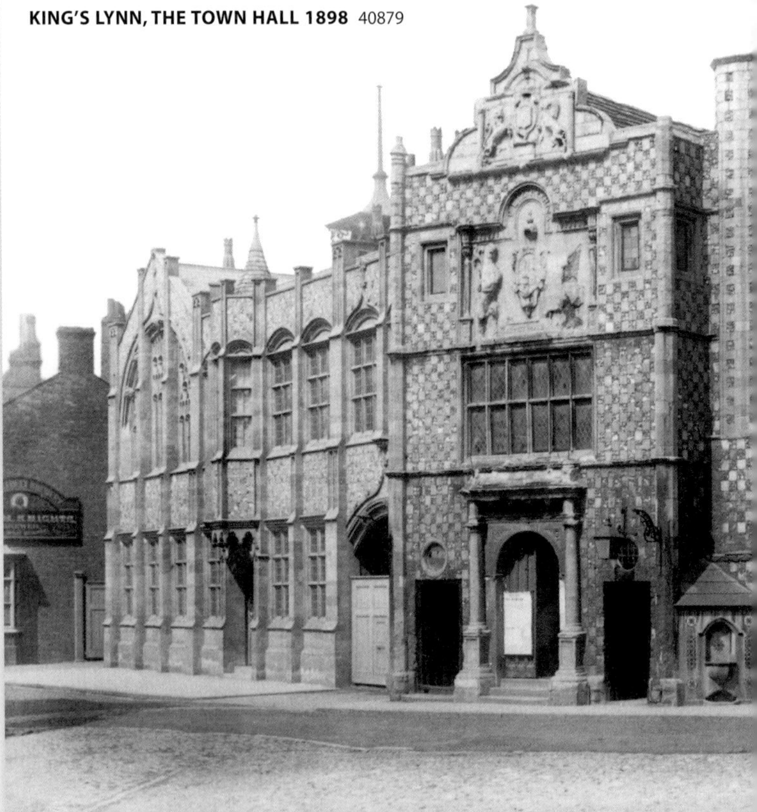

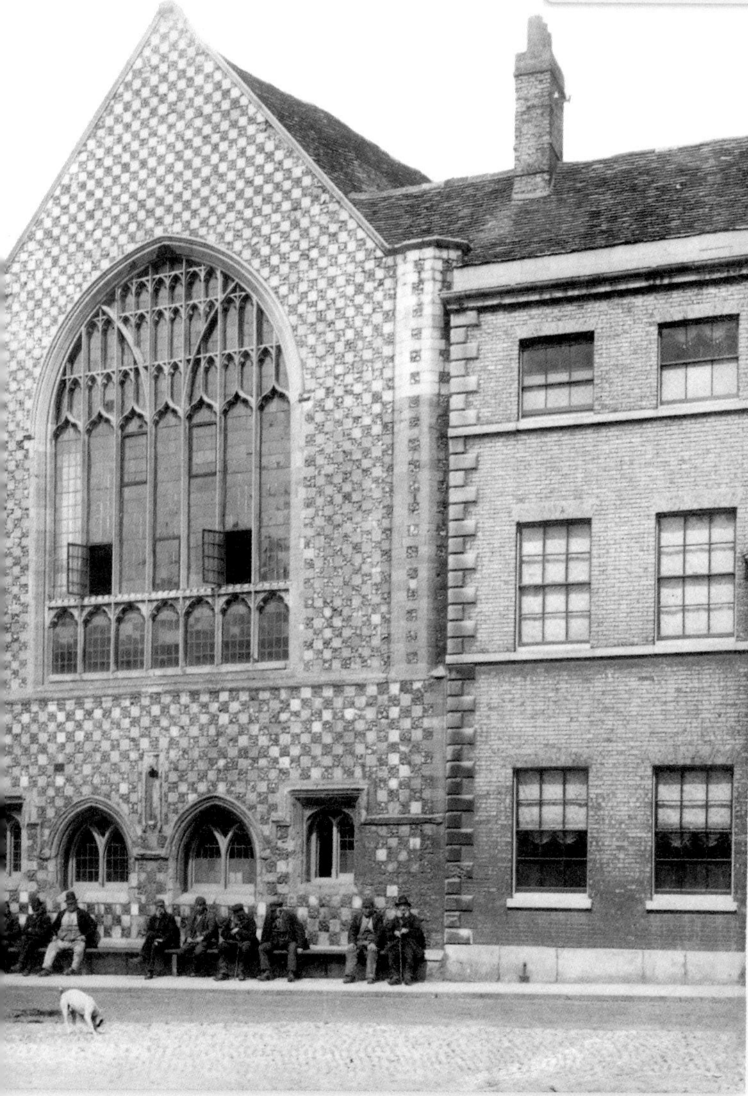

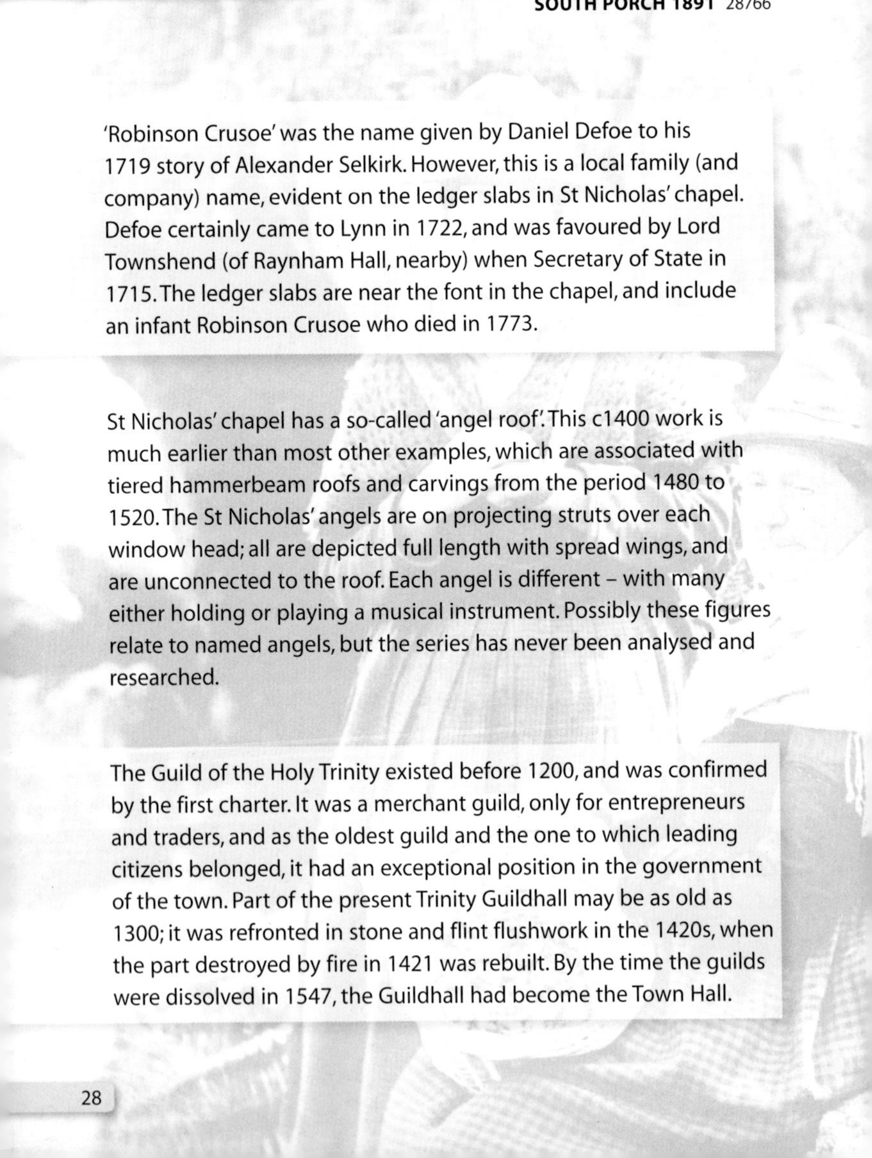

KING'S LYNN, ST NICHOLAS' CHAPEL, SOUTH PORCH 1891 28766

'Robinson Crusoe' was the name given by Daniel Defoe to his 1719 story of Alexander Selkirk. However, this is a local family (and company) name, evident on the ledger slabs in St Nicholas' chapel. Defoe certainly came to Lynn in 1722, and was favoured by Lord Townshend (of Raynham Hall, nearby) when Secretary of State in 1715. The ledger slabs are near the font in the chapel, and include an infant Robinson Crusoe who died in 1773.

St Nicholas' chapel has a so-called 'angel roof'. This c1400 work is much earlier than most other examples, which are associated with tiered hammerbeam roofs and carvings from the period 1480 to 1520. The St Nicholas' angels are on projecting struts over each window head; all are depicted full length with spread wings, and are unconnected to the roof. Each angel is different – with many either holding or playing a musical instrument. Possibly these figures relate to named angels, but the series has never been analysed and researched.

The Guild of the Holy Trinity existed before 1200, and was confirmed by the first charter. It was a merchant guild, only for entrepreneurs and traders, and as the oldest guild and the one to which leading citizens belonged, it had an exceptional position in the government of the town. Part of the present Trinity Guildhall may be as old as 1300; it was refronted in stone and flint flushwork in the 1420s, when the part destroyed by fire in 1421 was rebuilt. By the time the guilds were dissolved in 1547, the Guildhall had become the Town Hall.

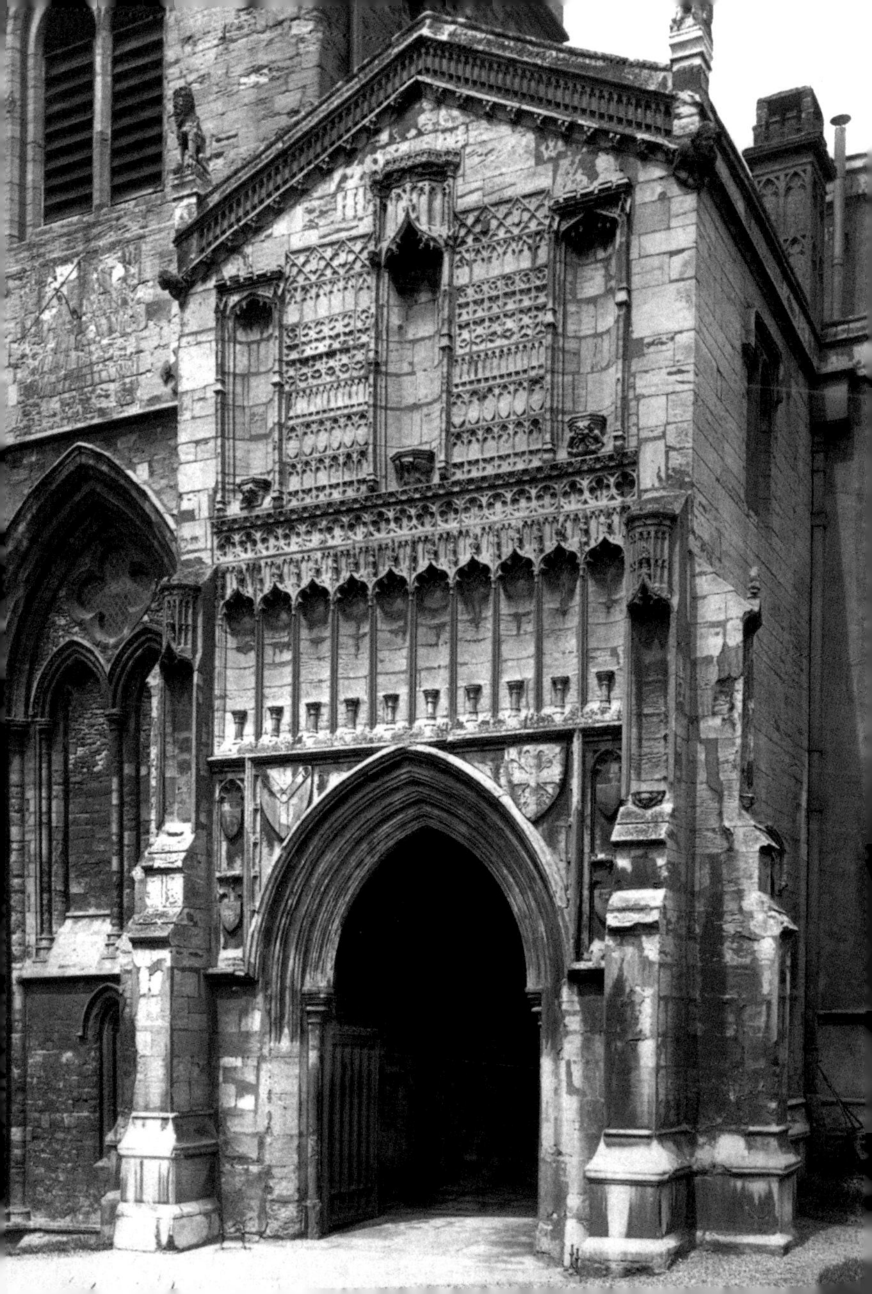

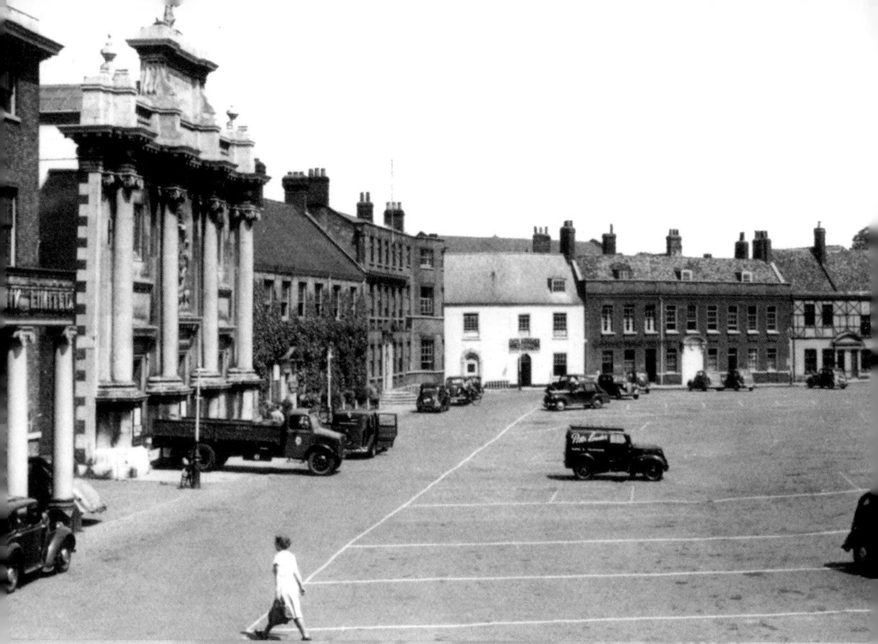

KING'S LYNN, TUESDAY MARKET PLACE c1955 K28037

Milling grain was difficult in Lynn. The first mills were water-powered, but the force of the water was sluggish, as on the Millfleet site beside Greyfriars. The first windmills were open trestle mills – such as shown on Robert Braunche's memorial brass in St Margaret's Church. The Red Mount was one position where windmills were tried out, as was South Lynn. In the 19th century tower mills were built with cap rings to move the sails round. There were tower mills at Gaywood Road and Wootton Road in Reffley, and a postmill at Fairstead.

Friar Nicholas of Lynn was a Franciscan who travelled and wrote. About 1360 he is said to have made an Arctic journey beyond Iceland, and to have reached Newfoundland or Greenland. He presented a treatise on his northern voyages to King Edward III, and then in 1386 made an astronomical calendar for the period to 1462. He was also known to Geoffrey Chaucer, and may have been the model for Nicholas in 'The Miller's Tale'.

KING'S LYNN, ROMAN ARCH 1921 71056

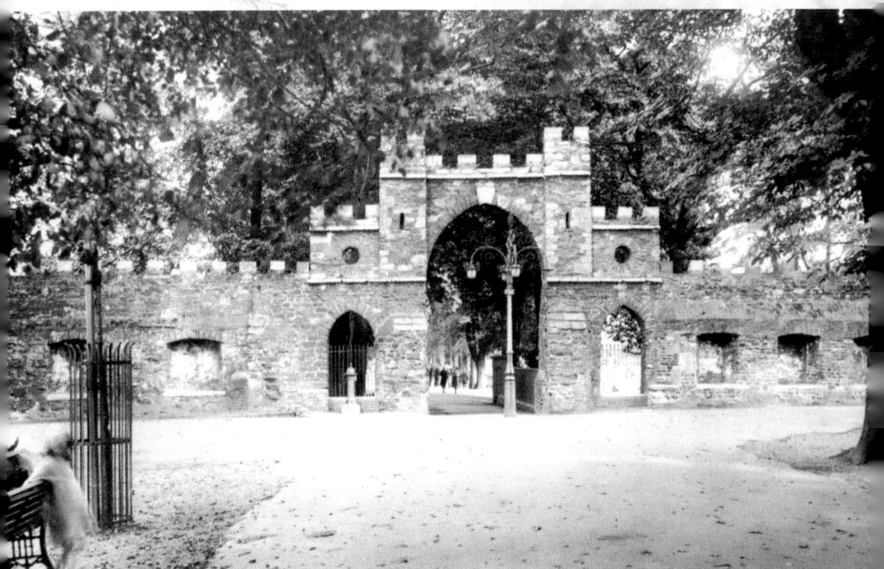

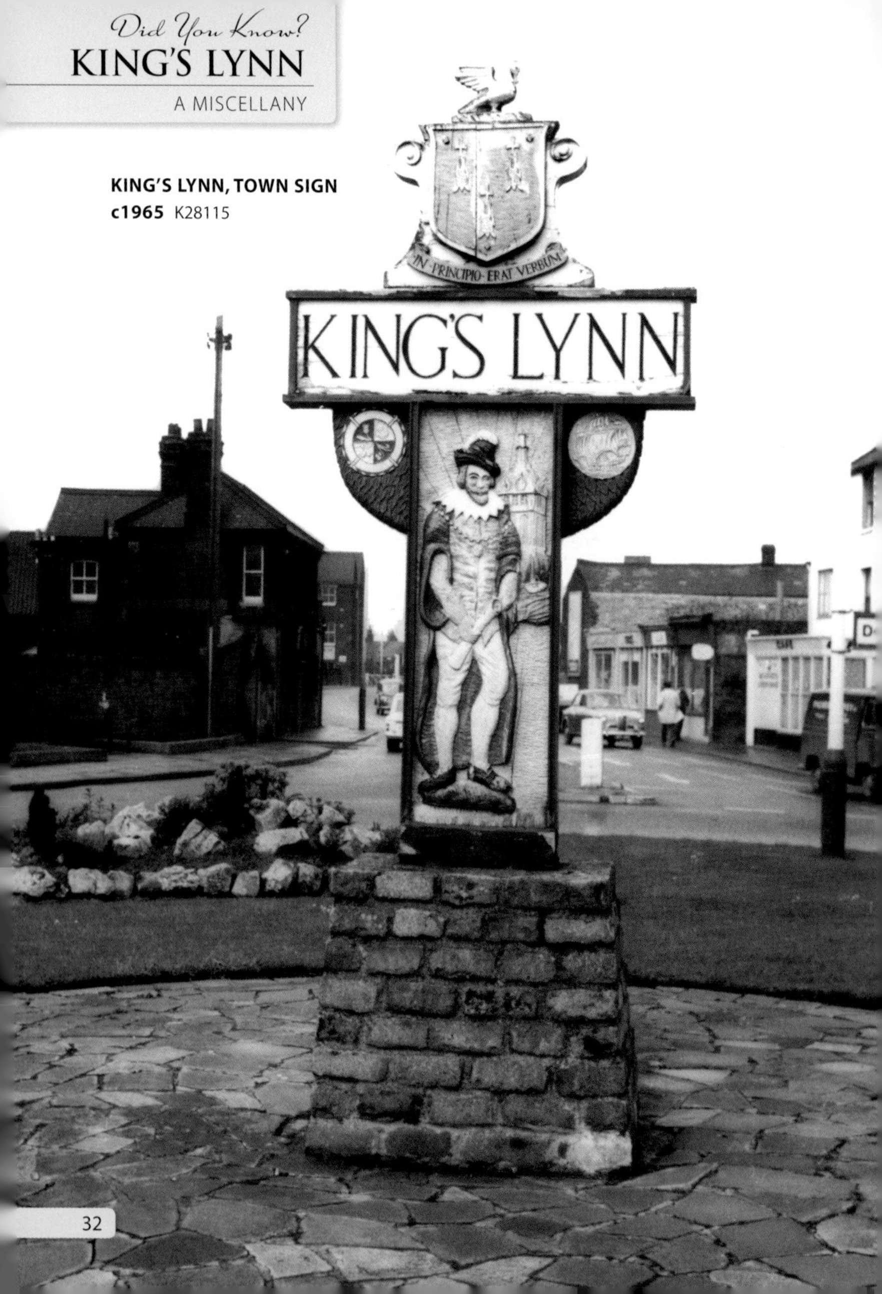

KING'S LYNN, TOWN SIGN c1965 K28115

Markets in the town were not limited to the two main market places, even though the Tuesday Market Place is almost 1 hectare (2.5 acres) in size. The Saturday market took place mainly along the street – today's open space was mostly part of the church itself, which had a double north aisle, a charnel chapel and the Trinity Guild chapel – or in the church yard. Norfolk Street included Grassmarket; St Nicholas' Street was formerly Woolmarket.

There was no market cross in these market places – market oaths, to seal bargains, were made at the adjacent churches if necessary. A market-cross building was erected on Tuesday Market in 1601, but its purpose was to provide a rest room for the beadles, and some permanent butchers' stalls. It was replaced by Henry Bell's tall and elaborate building of 1707. This was declared unsafe and removed (apparently with difficulty!) in 1829, and the materials auctioned. A gasolier – chandelier of lights lit by town gas – was the replacement feature, and this lasted until 1924.

The only King's Lynn holder of the Victoria Cross medal 'for valour' was John Shaul, born in Windsor Terrace in 1873. Because his father had been a soldier, John was able to go to the Duke of York's Army School in Chelsea. In 1898 he enlisted as a bandsman in the 1st Battalion, Highland Light Infantry (recruited mainly from Glasgow!). John's medal was awarded for giving First-Aid under fire at the Battle of Magersfontein, 11 December 1899, in the South African War. He never returned to King's Lynn, and after Army service until 1910 lived in South Africa.

KING'S LYNN, SOUTH GATES 1891 28759

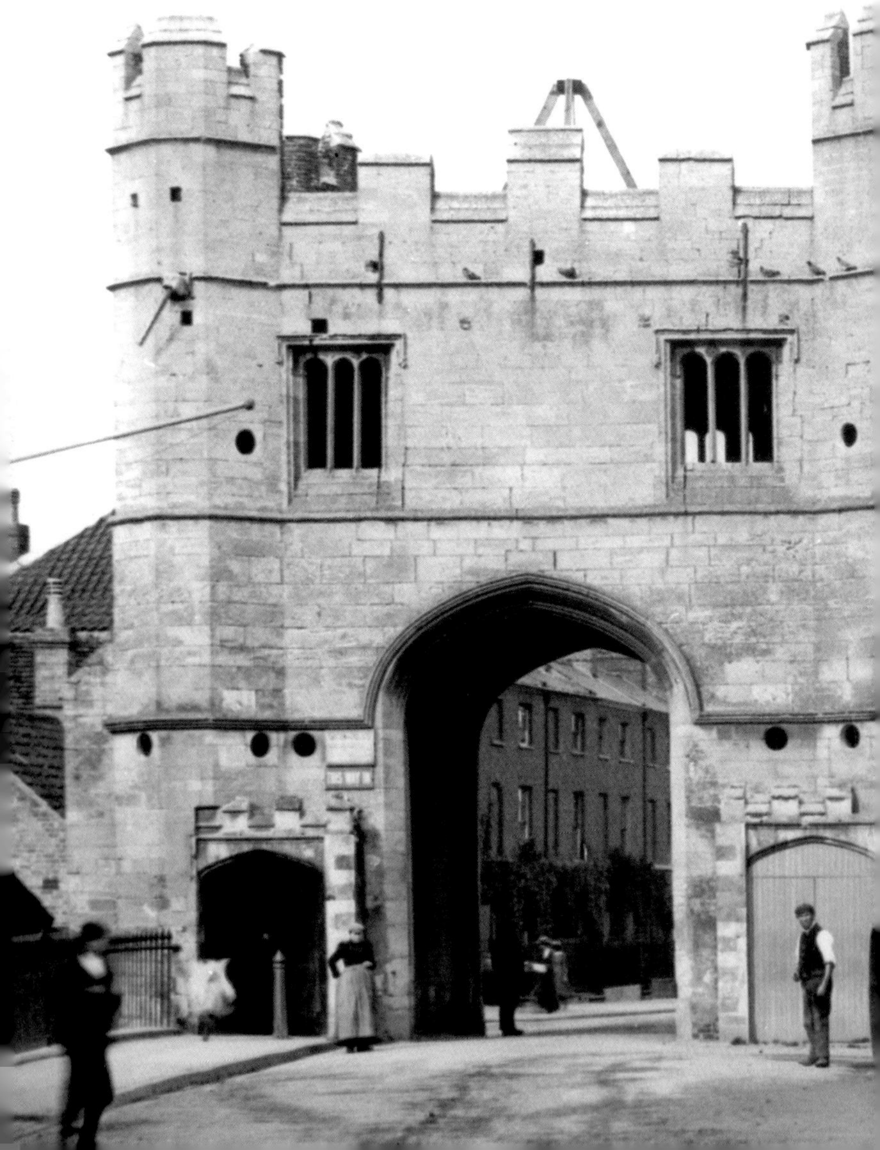

Bank House in King's Staithe Square is a jumble of history. Underneath, 15th-century brick vaults stretch out below the 1789 banking hall and in front of the house (built about 1685, with 18th- and early 19th-century alterations). Confusingly, the statue on the front parapet of Charles I (d 1649) was resited here in 1685, from the first Custom House (built in the Tuesday Market Place in 1630).

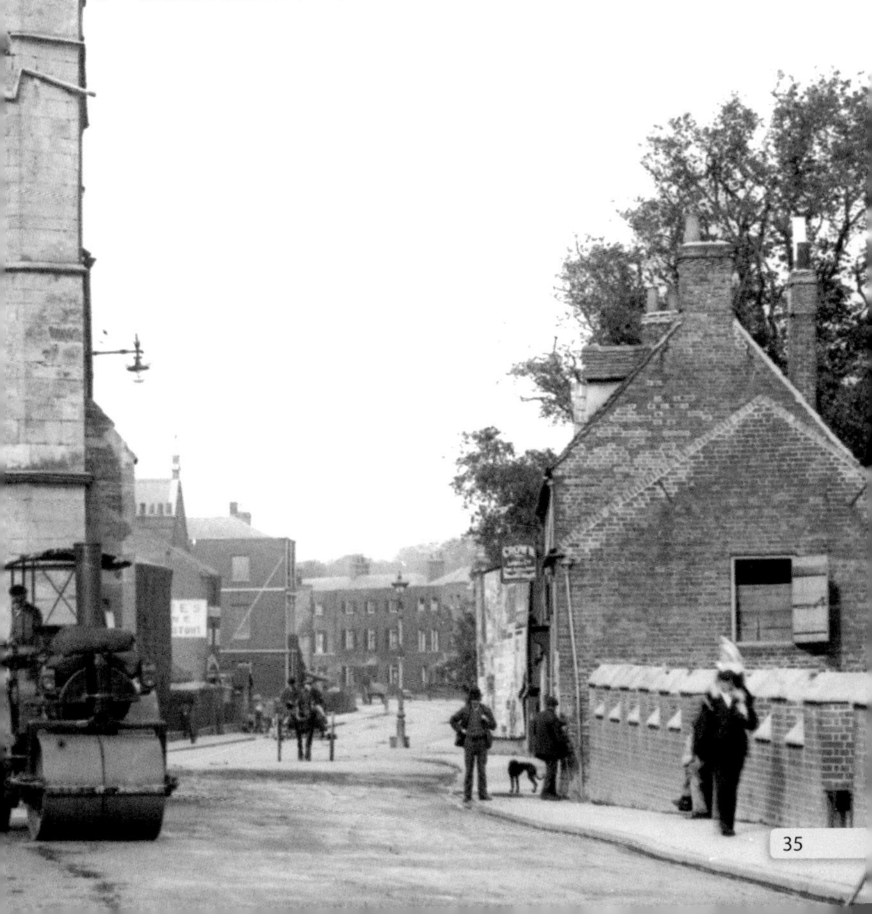

The second Custom House, with a statue of Charles II, was built in 1683 on an open quay beside the house of Sir John Turner. He paid for the building, which was like a market hall, open below, with a merchants' exchange (sale room) above. This idea was a failure, because the port trade was already focused at Tuesday Market Place and St Ann's. The Customs service bought the building in 1718, and used it as their port office until 1989.

The Green Quay museum is in Marriott's Barn (named after a Victorian corn and coal dealer). The walls include early 14th-century stonework and mid 16th-century bricks, with a brick cellar below. The work for the Millennium has rewritten the history of this building, which arose from a new wharf in the 1440s, and a building of about 1570 raised to the present size in about 1590. There was no Hanseatic connection, or separate island, as had been supposed.

The Majestic Cinema is one of the newest listed buildings. It was built in 1927 for a local company, and included two shops and a ballroom. It is an elaborate complex and has much surviving internal decoration and an unaltered Baroque exterior. Extra screens and more comfortable seats have been added in more recent times. Like the Theatre Royal, from the back it looks like a giant brick shed.

Thoresby College was being built when Thoresby died in 1510. The front gate is remarkable for being carved in 'parchment fold' panels – a Spanish style, reflecting Queen Katharine of Aragon, rather than the usual English 'linenfold' style. Across the door are the words 'Orate pro anima Magistri Thome Thoresby fundatoris hujus loci' (Pray for the soul of Master Thomas Thoresby, founder of this place). The first three words were removed by Puritan reformers in the 1640s.

KING'S LYNN, GREY FRIARS TOWER
1891 28768

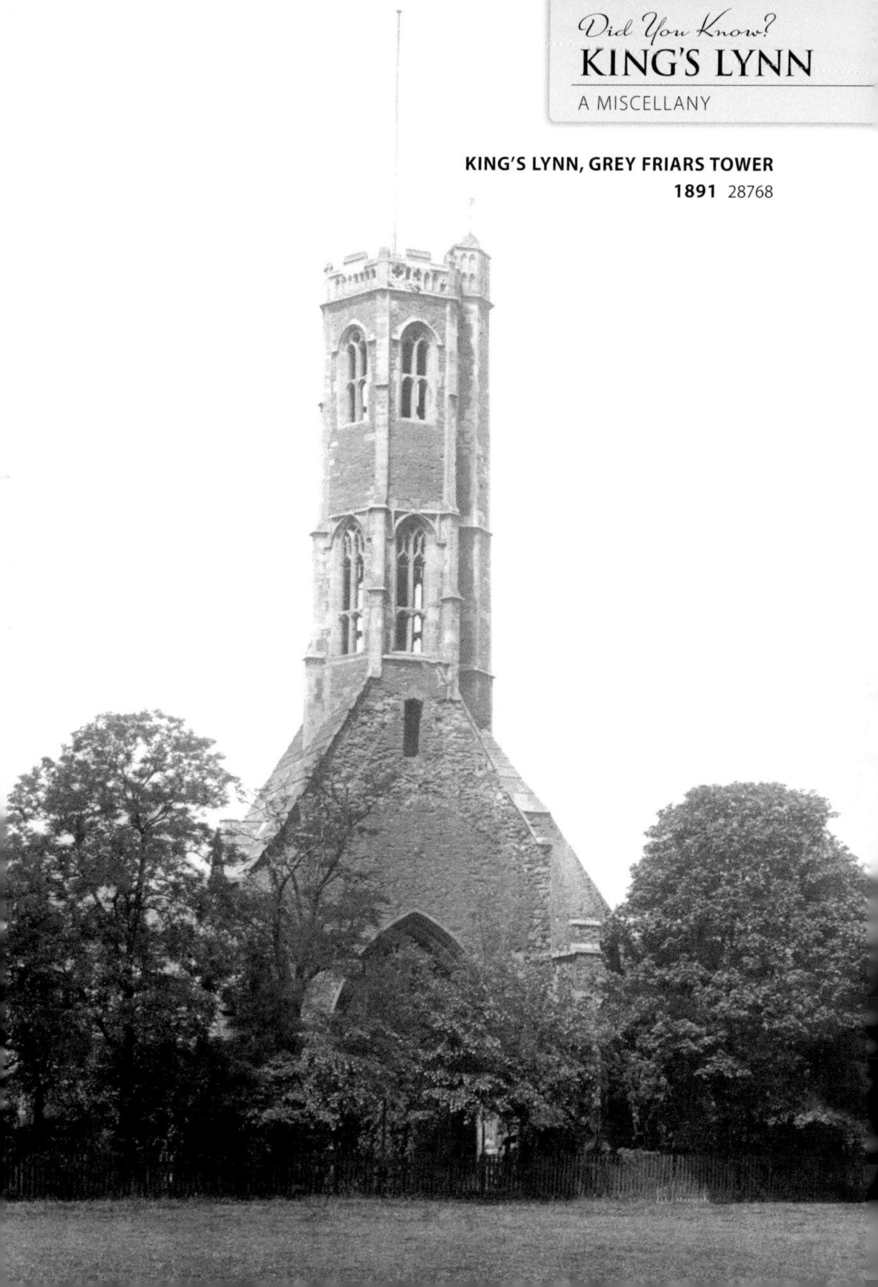

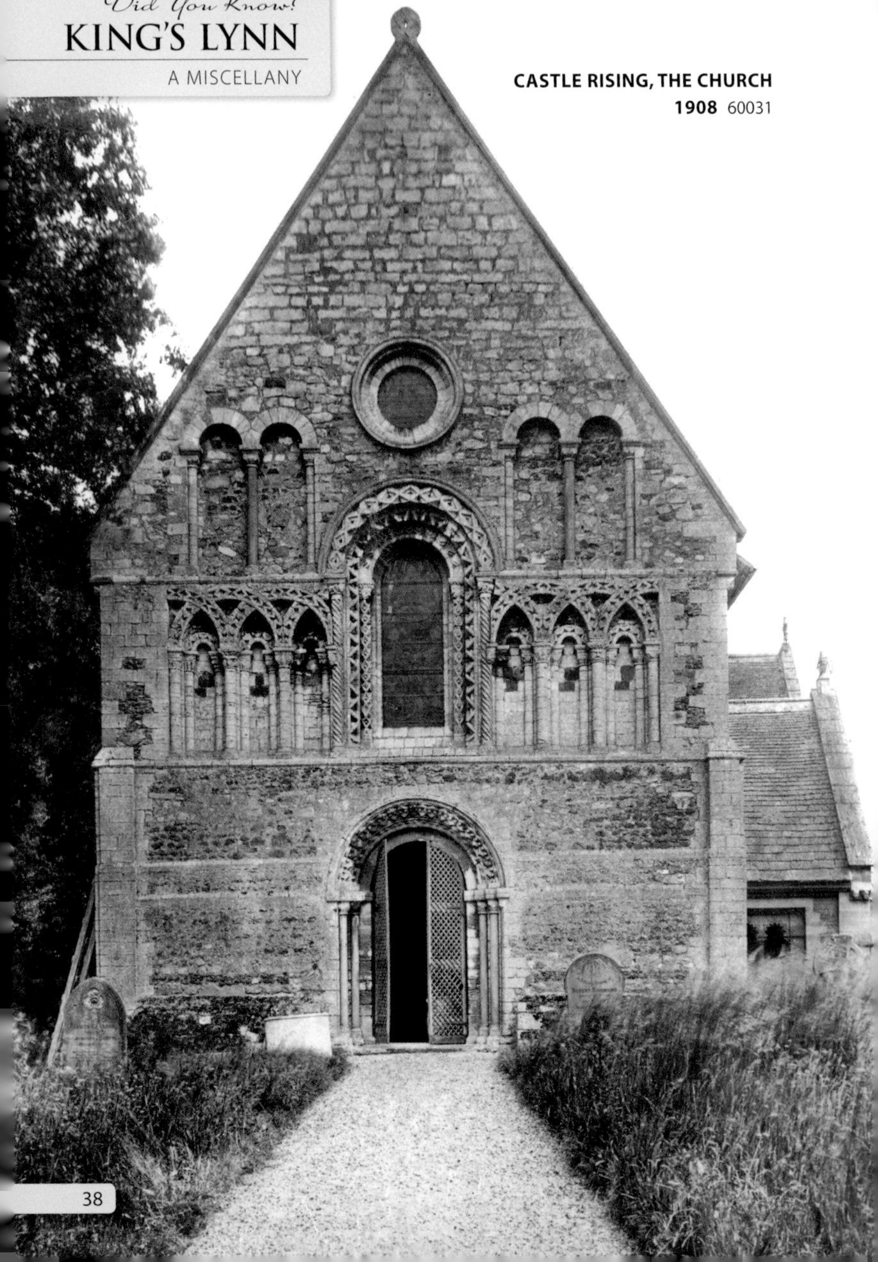

CASTLE RISING, THE CHURCH
1908 60031

Henry Bell (1647–1711) has often been suggested as the architect of any stylish building in the area! His father was a merchant dealing in corn, but also importing North European pictures. Henry went on Tour in the Netherlands, and was appointed to rebuild Northampton after a fire in 1675. He was a Lynn councillor, mayor in 1692 and 1703, inherited his father's business in 1686, and lived at the house that is now LloydsTSB bank at 23 High Street.

The Bagge family, now living at Stradsett Hall south of Lynn, have the most remarkable record of work and service in the town. The name is known from 1165, and the family provided 13 mayors between 1739 and 1837 alone. By then their town homes on Tuesday Market Place and Nelson Street were being replaced by country estates at Gaywood, Islington and Stradsett. The brewery at 10 King Street was Bagge's from 1686 to 1929.

Sir Benjamin Keene (1697–1757) was the son of a mercer in Lynn, but a diplomat in Lisbon and Madrid for 26 years at a time when Britain was developing world-wide commercial links. He was knighted (KB) for his services as ambassador in Madrid in 1754 – at that time an extremely rare honour for a person not of noble status. His monument in St Nicholas' chapel is a marble urn, from a design by Robert Adam, with a scene from Lisbon and the Order of the Bath carved on it.

In 1588 all leading ports were called on to supply ships to fight with Francis Drake in the English Channel, but most Lynn ships were already at sea. The 'Mayflower', a 150-ton coasting vessel, was sent that year, and five or six others in 1589, to harry the Spanish Armada as it sailed north round Scotland to try and escape back to Spain.

Town Improvement Commissioners replaced the Parish Vestry, to alter streets and bridges. The King's Lynn Paving Acts of 1803 and 1806, the first in Norfolk, could levy rates on properties, and lasted until 1872. Streets were set to 'building lines', with compensation for properties set back and corners rounded, in the distinctive brown Wisbech brick. Streets were paved in Aberdeen granite setts, Caithness flags or York stone, with Spurn Head pebbles, and the first pavements were created.

There are printed engravings of the 'Festival for the Return of Peace' that took place in July 1814 – before Napoleon started the Waterloo campaign. The entire Tuesday Market Place was taken over for a huge dinner for the town's 5,963 inhabitants, mostly paid for by private subscriptions from the merchant families. They ate 8 bullocks and 430 plum puddings, and consumed 41 barrels of beer. South Lynn residents feasted separately, in a field near South Gates.

In Millfleet there is still a walled Jewish cemetery, the surviving remnant of an early 19th-century Anglo-Dutch community. It was last used in 1848. Up until the 1860s the name Jews Lane was a reminder of the commercial role played by Jews in Lynn. It is now known as Surrey Street. The original Jewish community from c1150 was massacred in February 1190, after sacrilegious rumours were brought from Norwich.

Bad sanitation was the cause of high death rates and outbreaks of smallpox, cholera and typhoid in the town as late as 1897. At that time wooden waterpipes, 'night soil' boxes in tenements, and brick drains with no water flow were still widespead. 'A nasty stinking sinkhole of sin, which the map of the county denotes as Lynn.' Up until 1853 the Great Ouse tidal bore, known as the eager, could not scour into the fleets, and drains to the river were limited to the new paved streets.

CASTLE RISING, THE CASTLE 1898 40894

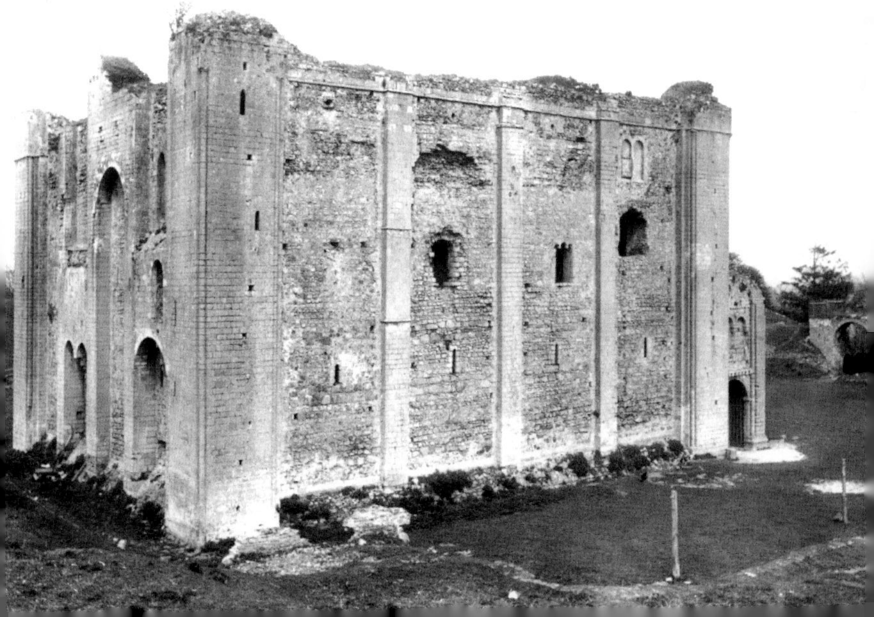

SPORTING KING'S LYNN

Lynn has produced an England Test Cricketer, Peter Howard Parfitt, who attended King Edward VII Grammar School in King's Lynn. He played for Middlesex CCC between 1956 and 1972, captaining the 1st XI from 1968 to 1970. He played in 37 Tests for England between 1962 and 1972.

King's Lynn Football Club is nicknamed 'The Linnets'. In the 2007-08 season the club became champions of the Southern League Premier Division. The Linnets have an impressive record in the FA Cup, having won the most games in the tournament in terms of games played against games won, and are seventh in the list of all time goals scored in the tournament, just three goals behind Manchester United. The club's highest ever win was in 1930, when they beat Beccles 17-0; their worst defeat was in the 1905-06 FA Cup when they lost 0-11 to Aston Villa. The Linnet's list of record holders includes Mick Wright - 1,152 career appearances (a British record), Malcolm Lindsay - career goal scorer with 321 goals, and George Martin - goals in a season (for 1909-10, scoring 69 goals from 38 appearances).

The King's Lynn Stars are the town's motorcycle speedway team. The team has been known variously as The Knights, The Silver Machine and The Stars. 2006 was a good year for The Stars, who not only won the Premier League Championship but also won the Premier Trophy and the 2006 Premier Knock-out Cup. They almost repeated the treble in 2007, once again winning the Premier Trophy and Premier League Knock-out Cup, but lost the league championship in the play-off semi-final to the Sheffield Tigers, despite finishing top of the Premier League table.

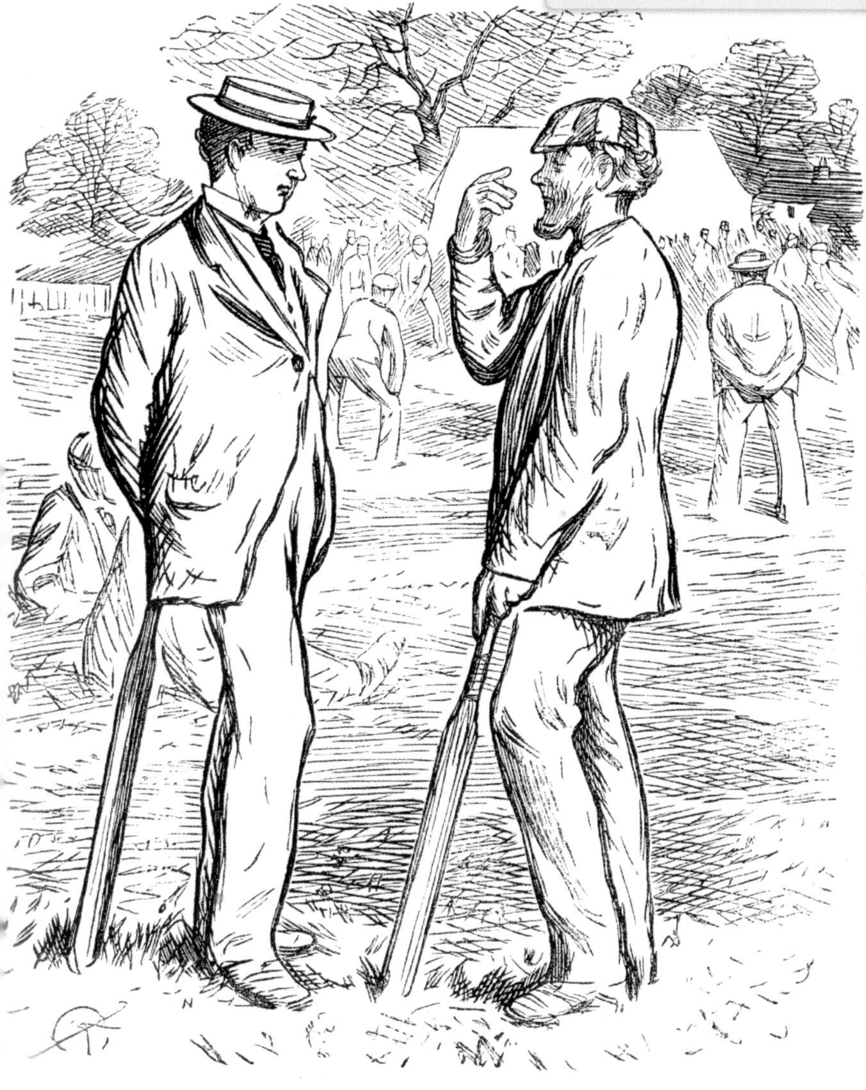

QUIZ QUESTIONS

Answers on page 50.

1. What does the word 'Lynn' in the town's name mean?

2. King's Lynn was not always the name of the town - by what name was it formerly known?

3. A statue of a Roman goddess stands at the top of the Corn Exchange in Lynn. Who is she?

4. Whereabouts in Lynn can you find an earthwork from the time of the Civil War siege of the town in the 17th century?

5. What was the connection between Sir Robert Walpole, Britain's first Prime Minister, and Lynn?

6. Why were local schoolchildren organised to collect conkers in 1917, during the First World War?

7. Why is there a road in Lynn named after the American president John F Kennedy?

8. Lynn had the misfortune to be one of very few British towns to suffer what during the First World War?

9. What is the link between Lynn and Pocahontas, the Native American princess famous in history for an act of mercy?

10. On 25 January 1945 the Town Hall at Lynn was the subject of a royal visit known as 'the visit of the three queens'. Who were the royal ladies involved?

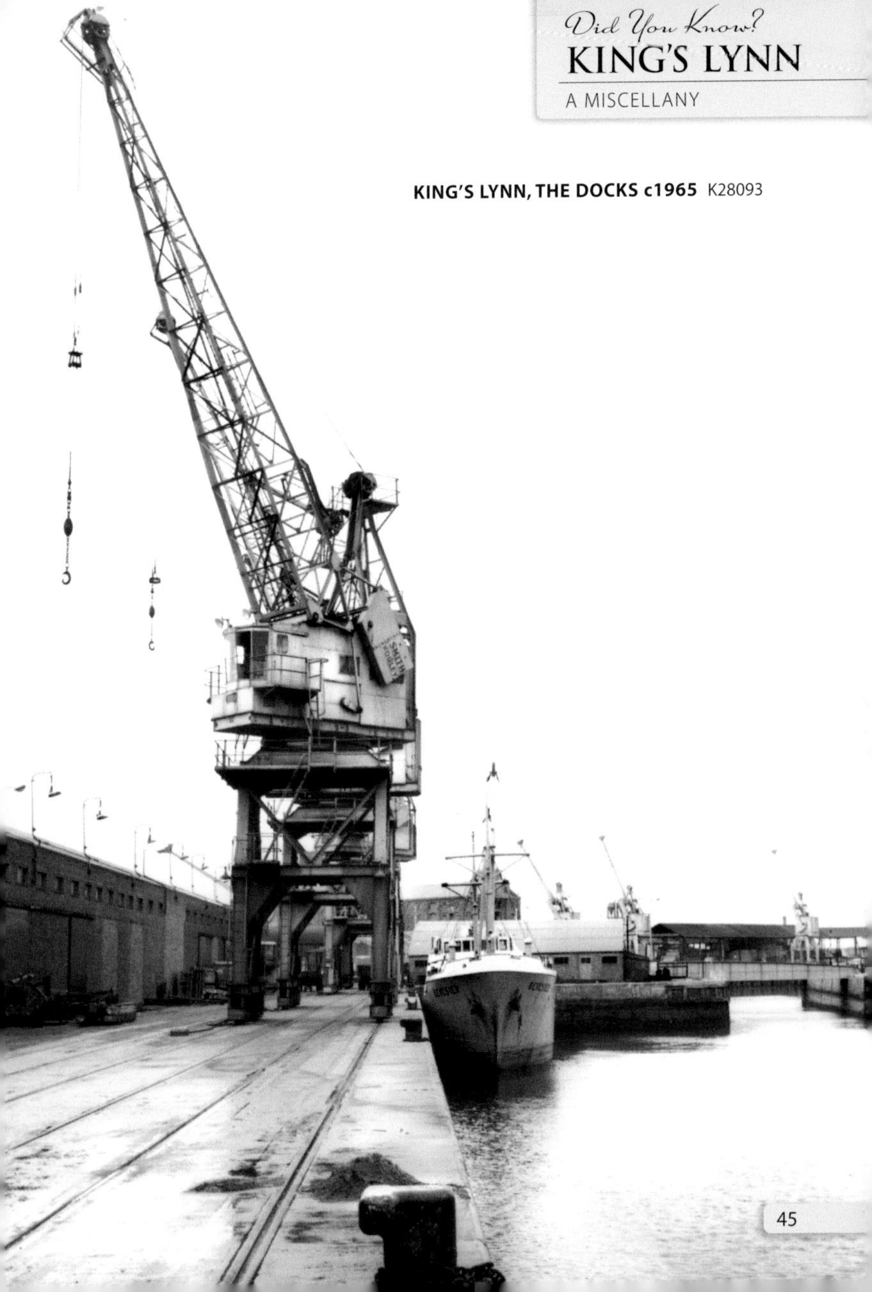

KING'S LYNN, THE DOCKS c1965 K28093

RECIPE

NELSON SQUARES

This recipe recalls one of West Norfolk's most famous sons, Admiral Lord Nelson, who was born at Burnham Thorpe near Lynn in 1758. Replace the mixed peel with an extra 50g/2oz of dried fruit, if preferred.

Ingredients

225g/8oz stale white bread, with crusts removed
300ml/ ½ pint milk
115g/4oz currants or raisins, or a mixture of both
50g/2oz mixed peel, finely chopped
50g/2oz suet
50g/2oz demerara sugar
1-2 level teaspoonfuls mixed spice, to taste
1 egg for the mixture
500g/1lb shortcrust pastry or puff pastry
1 beaten egg or a little extra milk for sealing and glazing the pastry

Soak the bread in the milk for half an hour, then beat out any lumps to leave a smooth mixture. Add the dried fruit, mixed peel, suet, sugar and mixed spice and mix well. Mix in the egg, and add a little extra milk if the mixture is too stiff to spread easily.

Pre-heat the oven to 180°C/350°F/Gas Mark 4. Grease a deep 22cm/9 inch-square baking tin. Roll out the pastry and cut into two sections, making one approx 28cm/11 inches square, and the other approx 22cm/9 inches square. Use the bigger section to line the base of the baking tin - the pastry should come up the sides of the tin. Spread the fruit mixture evenly over the pastry in the tin, leaving a slight gap around the sides. Brush the edge of the pastry with some of the beaten egg or milk, cover the mixture with the other square of pastry and pinch the edges together with the bottom layer to seal them together and enclose the mixture. Brush the surface with milk or beaten egg and prick some holes in the surface with a fork. Bake in the oven for 1½ to 2 hours, until the pastry is golden brown. Leave to cool in the tin then turn out, sprinkle with sugar and cut into squares before serving.

RECIPE

PLUM PUDDING

St Ann's Fort, off North Street, is now just a square beside the Port offices. It was built as a gun battery protecting the river in 1570, and re-armed in 1626. Guns were replaced here with each threat of war, and stood from 1778 to the 1830s. In 1778 the Lynn volunteers joined by reciting an oath beginning 'That you will always prefer roast beef, plum pudding and good English beer, to soup maigre, fricassed frog and French wines ....'

Ingredients

100g/4oz fresh breadcrumbs
100g/4oz plain flour
100g/4oz suet
100g/4oz soft brown sugar
1 heaped teaspoonful of baking powder
100g/4oz mixed dried fruit
1 teaspoonful ground mixed spice
A small amount of milk, to mix

Put all the ingredients in a bowl and mix well, adding enough milk to form a stiff dough.

Sprinkle a clean pudding cloth or tea towel with a little flour. Shape the dough into a thick roll and place on the cloth, leaving a pleat of material at each end. Roll up the dough in the cloth and tie each end securely with string, and also tie it loosely around the centre to help the pudding keep its shape. Put the pudding into a large pan of boiling water and boil for 1½ hours, topping up the pan with more boiling water when necessary - take care not to allow it to boil dry. When the pudding is cooked, remove it from the pan, cut the string and remove the cloth and turn out the pudding onto a warmed dish. Serve with cream or custard, and also a little golden syrup if liked.

KING'S LYNN, HIGH STREET 1908 60023

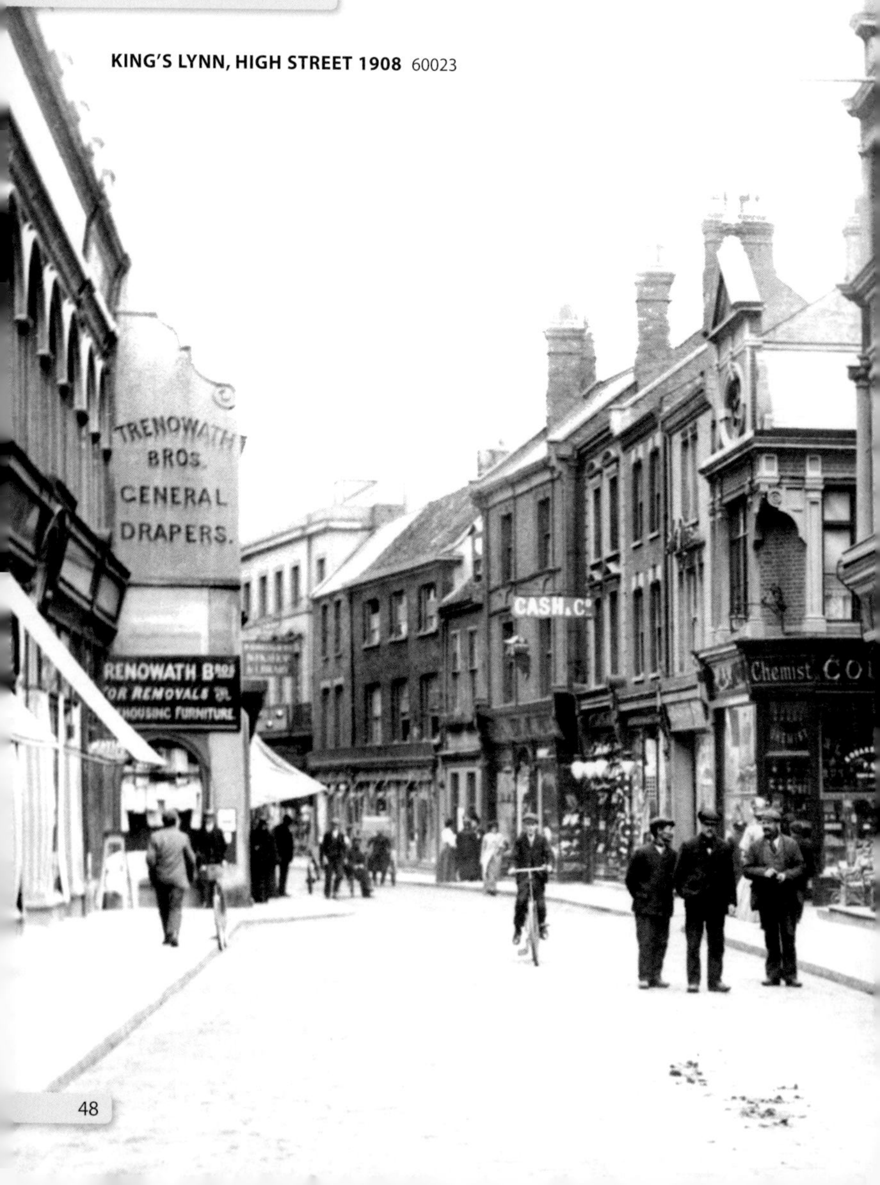

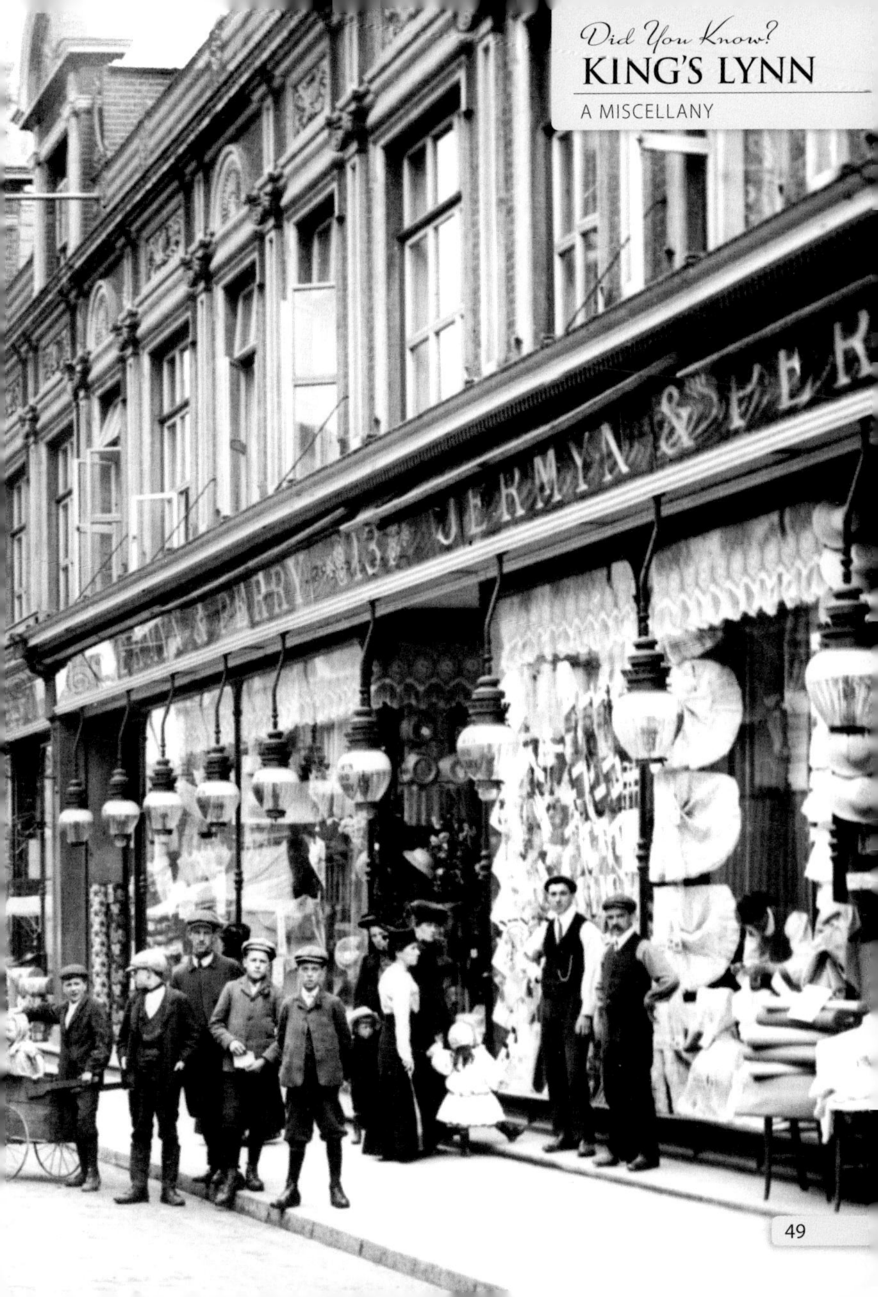
13
JERMYN

QUIZ ANSWERS

Questions on page 44.

1. It is derived from a Celtic word for a pool or lake.

2. The town of Lynn was founded by Herbert, Bishop of Norwich, around 1100; it was known as Bishop's Lynn until it passed from the Church to the Crown during the reign of Henry VIII.

3. A statue of Ceres, the Roman goddess of agriculture, grain, harvest and plenty, stands at the top of the Corn Exchange.

4. At Long Ponds, Loke Road.

5. Sir Robert Walpole (1676-1745) was also the MP for Lynn for 40 years.

6. To take to the government factory at the docks which produced acetone, derived from the conkers, for use in munitions. An estimated 3,000 tons were collected locally.

7. An American firm, Dow Agro-chemicals, opened a plant in the town just after John F Kennedy had been elected President in 1960.

8. Lynn was one of the few towns in Britain to be bombed from the air when it was attacked by a German Zeppelin on 9th January 1915, and two people were killed in Bentinck Street (now beneath the Clough Lane car park).The Savage's Iron Works, where aeroplane parts were made, was probably the target.

9. The Native American princess Pocahontas is famous in history for saving the life of Captain John Smith during the early settlement of Jamestown in Virginia, by throwing herself over his body to prevent him being clubbed to death by her father's warriors. Captain Smith had an eventful life, and as a young lad he worked for a year in Lynn as a merchant's apprentice.

10. The Town Hall was visited by Queen Mary, the widow of George V, Queen Elizabeth, the consort of George VI, and her daughter Princess Elizabeth, the future Queen Elizabeth II.

KING'S LYNN, RED MOUNT CHAPEL c1955 K28004

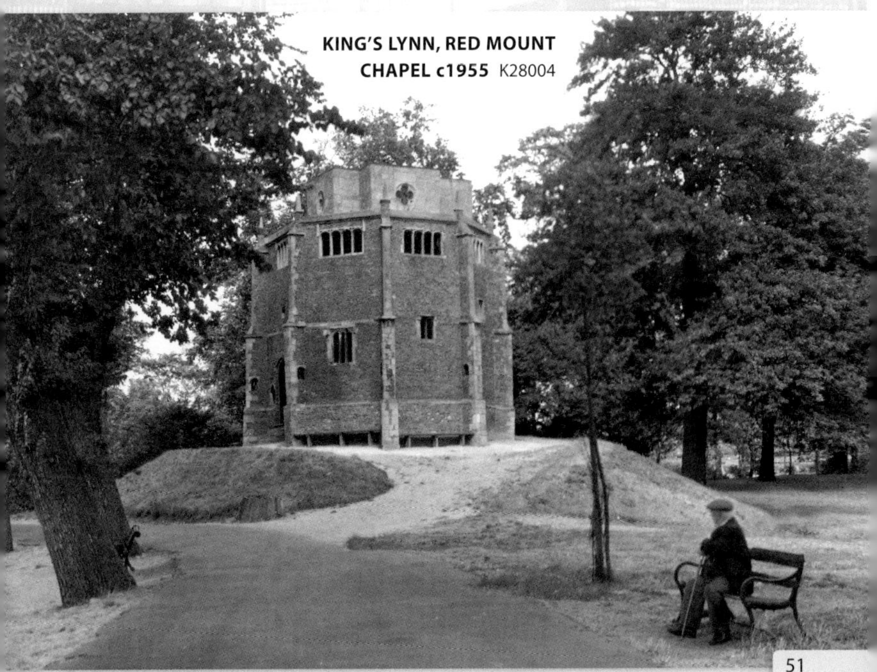

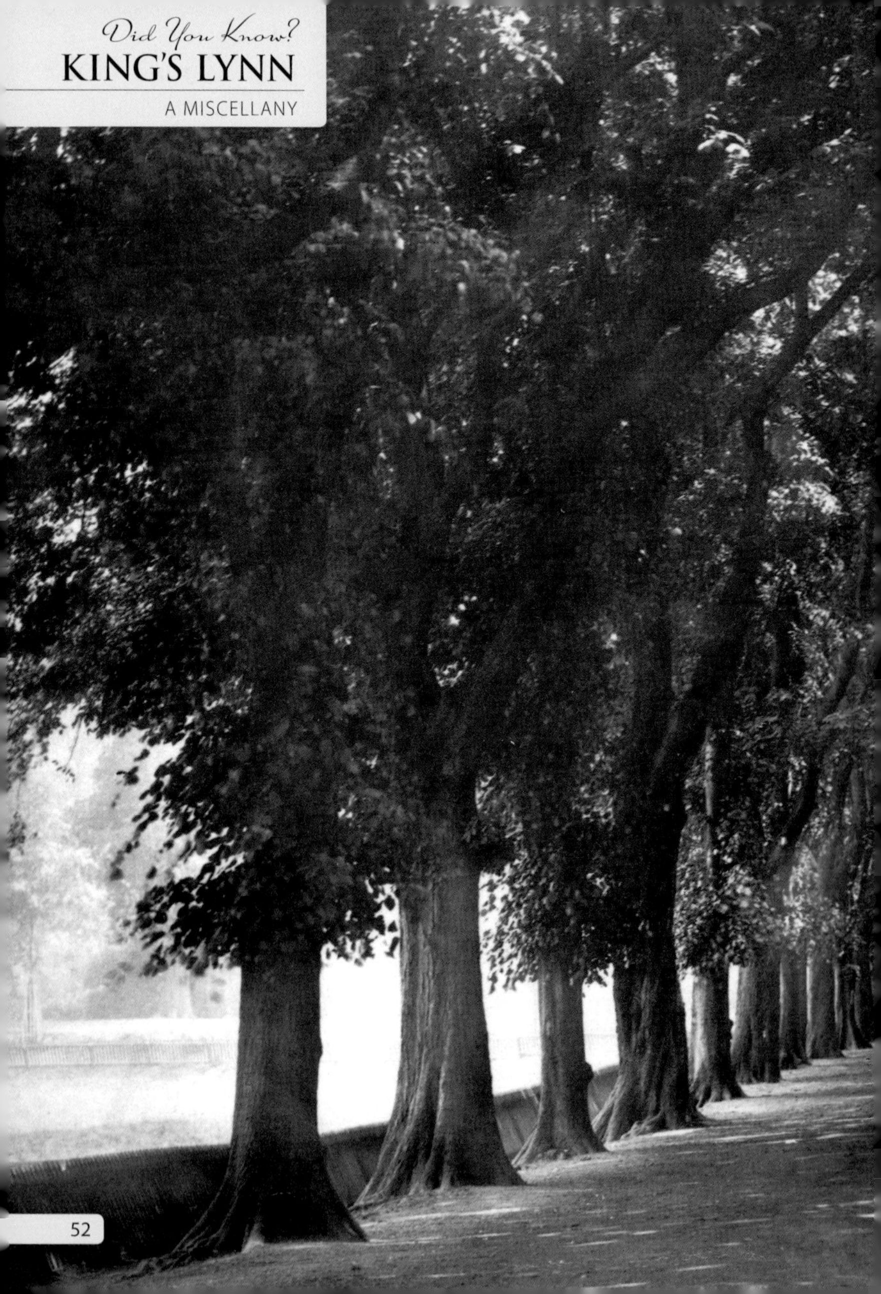

KING'S LYNN, THE BROAD WALKS 1891 28756

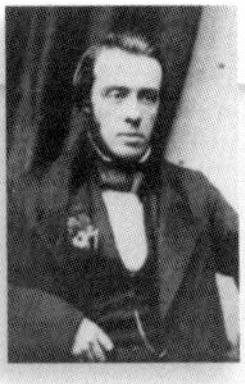

FRANCIS FRITH

PIONEER VICTORIAN PHOTOGRAPHER

Francis Frith, founder of the world-famous photographic archive, was a complex and multi-talented man. A devout Quaker and a highly successful Victorian businessman, he was philosophical by nature and pioneering in outlook. By 1855 he had already established a wholesale grocery business in Liverpool, and sold it for the astonishing sum of £200,000, which is the equivalent today of over £15,000,000. Now in his thirties, and captivated by the new science of photography, Frith set out on a series of pioneering journeys up the Nile and to the Near East.

INTRIGUE AND EXPLORATION

He was the first photographer to venture beyond the sixth cataract of the Nile. Africa was still the mysterious 'Dark Continent', and Stanley and Livingstone's historic meeting was a decade into the future. The conditions for picture taking confound belief. He laboured for hours in his wicker dark-room in the sweltering heat of the desert, while the volatile chemicals fizzed dangerously in their trays. Back in London he exhibited his photographs and was 'rapturously cheered' by members of the Royal Society. His reputation as a photographer was made overnight.

VENTURE OF A LIFE-TIME

By the 1870s the railways had threaded their way across the country, and Bank Holidays and half-day Saturdays had been made obligatory by Act of Parliament. All of a sudden the working man and his family were able to enjoy days out, take holidays, and see a little more of the world.

With typical business acumen, Francis Frith foresaw that these new tourists would enjoy having souvenirs to commemorate their days out. For the next thirty years he travelled the country by train and by pony and trap, producing fine photographs of seaside resorts and beauty spots that were keenly bought by millions of Victorians. These prints were painstakingly pasted into family albums and pored over during the dark nights of winter, rekindling precious memories of summer excursions. Frith's studio was soon supplying retail shops all over the country, and by 1890 F Frith & Co had become the greatest specialist photographic publishing company in the world, with over 2,000 sales outlets, and pioneered the picture postcard.

FRANCIS FRITH'S LEGACY

Francis Frith had died in 1898 at his villa in Cannes, his great project still growing. By 1970 the archive he created contained over a third of a million pictures showing 7,000 British towns and villages.

Frith's legacy to us today is of immense significance and value, for the magnificent archive of evocative photographs he created provides a unique record of change in the cities, towns and villages throughout Britain over a century and more. Frith and his fellow studio photographers revisited locations many times down the years to update their views, compiling for us an enthralling and colourful pageant of British life and character.

We are fortunate that Frith was dedicated to recording the minutiae of everyday life. For it is this sheer wealth of visual data, the painstaking chronicle of changes in dress, transport, street layouts, buildings, housing and landscape that captivates us so much today, offering us a powerful link with the past and with the lives of our ancestors.

Computers have now made it possible for Frith's many thousands of images to be accessed almost instantly. The archive offers every one of us an opportunity to examine the places where we and our families have lived and worked down the years. Its images, depicting our shared past, are now bringing pleasure and enlightenment to millions around the world a century and more after his death.

For further information visit: www.francisfrith.com

INTERIOR DECORATION

Frith's photographs can be seen framed and as giant wall murals in thousands of pubs, restaurants, hotels, banks, retail stores and other public buildings throughout Britain. These provide interesting and attractive décor, generating strong local interest and acting as a powerful reminder of gentler days in our increasingly busy and frenetic world.

FRITH PRODUCTS

All Frith photographs are available as prints and posters in a variety of different sizes and styles. In the UK we also offer a range of other gift and stationery products illustrated with Frith photographs, although many of these are not available for delivery outside the UK – see our web site for more information on the products available for delivery in your country.

THE INTERNET

Over 100,000 photographs of Britain can be viewed and purchased on the Frith web site. The web site also includes memories and reminiscences contributed by our customers, who have personal knowledge of localities and of the people and properties depicted in Frith photographs. If you wish to learn more about a specific town or village you may find these reminiscences fascinating to browse. Why not add your own comments if you think they would be of interest to others? See **www.francisfrith.com**

PLEASE HELP US BRING FRITH'S PHOTOGRAPHS TO LIFE

Our authors do their best to recount the history of the places they write about. They give insights into how particular towns and villages developed, they describe the architecture of streets and buildings, and they discuss the lives of famous people who lived there. But however knowledgeable our authors are, the story they tell is necessarily incomplete.

Frith's photographs are so much more than plain historical documents. They are living proofs of the flow of human life down the generations. They show real people at real moments in history; and each of those people is the son or daughter of someone, the brother or sister, aunt or uncle, grandfather or grandmother of someone else. All of them lived, worked and played in the streets depicted in Frith's photographs.

We would be grateful if you would give us your insights into the places shown in our photographs: the streets and buildings, the shops, businesses and industries. Post your memories of life in those streets on the Frith website: what it was like growing up there, who ran the local shop and what shopping was like years ago; if your workplace is shown tell us about your working day and what the building is used for now. Read other visitors' memories and reconnect with your shared local history and heritage. With your help more and more Frith photographs can be brought to life, and vital memories preserved for posterity, and for the benefit of historians in the future.

Wherever possible, we will try to include some of your comments in future editions of our books. Moreover, if you spot errors in dates, titles or other facts, please let us know, because our archive records are not always completely accurate—they rely on 140 years of human endeavour and hand-compiled records. You can email us using the contact form on the website.

Thank you!

For further information, trade, or author enquiries please contact us at the address below:

The Francis Frith Collection, Frith's Barn, Teffont, Salisbury, Wiltshire, England SP3 5QP.

Tel: +44 (0)1722 716 376 Fax: +44 (0)1722 716 881

e-mail: sales@francisfrith.co.uk **www.francisfrith.com**